THAT'S ENTERTAINMENT!

Erik Mortensen

'kræk.dʒə:

Crackjaw Publishing
Guelph, ON
www.crackjawpublishing.com

Library and Archives Canada Cataloguing in Publication

Mortensen, Erik, 1987-
That's entertainment! / Erik Mortensen.

Plays.
ISBN 978-0-9782026-7-5

I. Title.

PS8626 O78 T48 2008   C812'.6   C2008-904334-0

Contents

Dedication

This anthology is dedicated to all the members of The Mainstreet Players, all the members of The Not So Grand Players, Paul McNamara and the members of The Haiti Held Hostage production. All of you have had a great and positive impact on my work in theatre, both behind the pen and on the stage. All of you are wonderful people and inspiring talents.

Introduction

So, what is the purpose behind this anthology? Why did I put these scripts together and, more importantly, who am I? Well, the title of this book is "That's Entertainment", and that sums up my goal. I hope the scripts entertain you. I hope some of them make you laugh, I hope some of them make you think, or maybe you can take something from one of the scripts that just makes you smile or provides you with your own inspiration. I believe strongly that writing and various texts can and do have an influence on the world and people around them. Do I hope to have an influence on you?

I don't know if I want to have an influence, and I certainly know that these scripts will not in any way change the world. All I hope is they will amuse, delight and possibly get you thinking about some of the different subjects they talk about. I think texts should be analyzed and explored, and I do believe many things can be learned from them, but I also feel that none of the messages can properly be received unless the person exploring the text is entertained by it. So, for me, the greatest success that could be achieved from this book is if you have a moment where you laugh out loud, or you genuinely feel sad or moved, or a certain script impresses a certain thought or inspires you to think some more about your own opinion on some issues and ideas raised in the plays. If you were entertained, then I will have achieved my goal.

I also have written some brief introductions to the scripts, talking about some various ideas in the script and some anecdotes and memories of some of the shows I have run and my experiences with theatre and perhaps some advice for any who may be interested. You can feel free to skip these entirely. I do not think of myself as a theatre master. I have just been doing it for quite sometime, and feel I have gained some experience that might be worth me sharing or that may give some of you a laugh.

I started being involved with shows when I was in Grade 1 and have been involved with close to forty productions for stage in my life and several for film. I have acted, written, directed, built sets, produced and ushered. It has been a lot of fun. I don't ever plan to stop. Two and a half years ago I started my own theatre company, *The Mainstreet Players,* and some of the plays in this book I have produced through it. It has been a huge learning experience so far, and I know it will continue to be. For more information on me, my company and my various works, please feel free to investigate my website:

www.erikwilliammortensen.com. It is the official home of *The Mainstreet Players*, where the line between dream and reality fades...
Enjoy!

SCANDALS AND SCHEMES

A note on *Scandals and Schemes*

This is the production I am currently running while putting this anthology together for publication. The main point I'd like to discuss in relation to this script is the process of change from script to stage, or at least how the process functions when I direct or produce. The first point that I feel needs to be acknowledged is that there will be change and a fair degree of it. Strangely enough, with the right director and cast brought together, the script can be the beginning of complete artistic freedom. My cast for *Scandals and Schemes* is absolutely fantastic. They are, in fact, the best cast I have ever worked with. It consists of Hayden Arnell - Leonard Butterfield, Rod Saunders - Rankin Rawlings, Samuel Turner - Benson Belch and myself - Arthur Checker.

As a director, if I have the right cast, I love to give them freedom in crafting the character and, once they have found their way, I let them take the lead when appropriate. After all, if they ever go too far, I can reel them back in. This tends to lead to a great deal of improvisation and a number of things will change and be added to the script. For instance, we have added in some small pieces of dialogue which do not appear in the published version. A couple of other points we altered from the published version are opening of Scene 2 and the opening of Act 2.

In the production, Scene 2 will open on the magistrate entering into the scene and discovering a cat, which he promptly kicks offstage. Act 2 opens with the Magistrate reading a clearly naughty book. He gets certain ideas, which are implied, but his robes prevent him from following through. All these different additions and ideas can add so much to a production. As a writer or director, you can never think that you have thought of everything. If you have the right cast, they will bring talent and ideas that you never would have perceived. It will all add together to make an even greater production. This cast is one of those great casts who are committed to their characters and production.

This production also marks a special point in the company, as it will be the first to set the standard and ideal with which I wish to push the company from here on. I want every show to have as committed and dedicated a cast and each production to hold the professionalism that this one holds. Most importantly, it is the first production where all the proceeds are going to charity, something which is very important to me. Every major production I run will be for charity, and often the smaller productions will be run to fund raise for a larger charity production, if not for a charity all on its own. My hope is every production, through raising money, through the charity, and (I can only hope) through the script itself sometimes, will help create positive social change.

Characters

Leonard "Leo" Butterfield:

> A quirky and ambitious law clerk who is unafraid to skirt the rules to get ahead. Luck often seems to favor him, and he possesses more wit than it appears at times.

Benson Belch:

> A close friend of Leo who is always found in varying degrees of a drunken stupor and quick to scheme and plot. Always looking for a good time and often finding trouble.

Arthur "Art" Checker:

> A pirate who is seeking revenge and property which used to be his. Often trigger happy and completely wily and untrustworthy.

Rankin Rawlings:

> A corrupt magistrate and a ruthless man who will stop at nothing to get what he wants. Cautious but also dangerous to cross.

Scandals and Schemes

ACT I

Scene I

Then scene opens on English pub in the 18th century. There is the sound of clinking glasses and quick tempo music in background. There is the sound of frivolity and celebration in the streets. There is a small wooden table with chairs, and Benson Belch is sitting at the table. In front of him is a wine bottle with glasses, and he is dressed in a masquerade costume with his mask on the table. The table is lit by candlelight, and this set is placed stage left. As Benson is enjoying his wine, another costume-clad figure enters the pub wearing a blue jester mask. When he takes off the mask, he reveals himself to be Leo Butterfield. Benson immediately recognizes his friend and heartily welcomes him to join him at the table. Leo does so and, as he sits, he takes the bottle of wine and pours himself a glass, then passes the battle back to Benson.

Leo: Tonight is a night of celebration my good man, Benson Belch.

Benson: Yes it is, I'll drink to that. (*Taking a swig of wine.*)

Leo: No, I mean for us.

Benson: I'll drink to that too! (*Takes another swig and belches.*) But how so?

Leo: Fortune smiles on us, and all because of this. (*Motions to the mask and the costume he has on.*)

Benson: It is a lovely costume, if not a bit out of your means, is it not Leo?

Leo: Completely out of my means. I never could afford it, but now it will make us a fortune.

Benson: I am not sure I entirely understand.

Leo: Oh, but you will soon enough. (*Taking another drink before he begins his excited explanation.*) As you know, for New Year the fashionable thing to do nowadays is to have a masquerade ball. Now everyone knows the greatest ball on New Year's Eve is the one held by the high society, the Earl Chutney's ball. Magistrate Rawlings attends it every year and always wears the same costume, this costume. (*Motioning about the one which he is wearing.*)

Benson: So, then the judge is running around naked?

Leo: No.

Benson: So he is just out of costume?

Leo: I don't know, but it is not pertinent to the story. May I continue?

Benson: (*Holds up his hand and takes another swig of wine.*) Go on.

Leo: Thank you. So, Magistrate Rawlings allowed me to borrow his costume and, since my costume would look far too fashionable for one of the balls we would normally attend, I decided to attend the Earl's ball in his stead. He didn't explain why he was unable to participate in any festivities, but I am glad he could not.

Benson: So, it was good party?

Leo: Hardly. Far too stuffy and not nearly enough drink.

Benson: I suppose you don't remain wealthy and drink largely. Still, I'd rather be broke and drunk than rich and sober.

Leo: Not altogether shocking, but back to the tale. So, I enter the Earl's party in the magistrate's costume, a reward for my hard work and a product of his busy schedule. Funny thing, as I entered the party, everyone there assumed I was the magistrate. Since I had on the mask and costume, they didn't know better. This played marvelously to my advantage.

Benson: Your story is beginning to bore me, and my bottle of wine is disappearing. Unless it picks up before I am finished, I will be forced to leave you in seek of more stimulating entertainment.

Leo: Then I'd better hurry, as I haven't much time.

Benson: (*Taking another swig.*) Indeed.

Leo: (*Getting up.*) Very well. (*Gets Benson up and positions him out from the table.*) You will be me at the party.

Benson: Except far better looking. And who will you be in this reenactment?

Leo: The woman who accosted me.

Benson: You are a woman; that is believable. The fact that she accosted you, and there was not free flowing wine at this party, that is not as believable.

Leo: (*Gives Benson a glare.*) At very least, I am sure the story is starting to become more entertaining.

Benson: We will see, when you actually start telling me what happened.

Leo: Very Well. So you, being me, was on the dance floor, and a number of people were greeting me with waves and smiles. Then a woman accosted me, in a very seductive manner. (*Walks to Benson.*)

Benson: You call that seductive? If you are going to act the part, at least act it right.

Leo: Very well. (*Approaches again, only this time acting seductively.*) The woman accosted me under the impression that I was the magistrate. I must say, between the way the dress hugged her snug around her figure and the delicious filth she was whispering, I really wished that I was the magistrate. (*Being seductive throughout.*)

Benson: I'm wishing you were the woman right now. (*Both stare at each other as they hold each other in a compromising position. The awkward moment breaks, and they straighten their clothes and clear their throats.*) Isn't the magistrate married?

Leo: Yes, to a hideous cow, but one with money. Clearly, though, this was not his wife.

Benson: Now that is intriguing. The pious magistrate was having an affair.

Leo: Oh, believe me, he is not so pious, and this letter bears that point out. (*Producing the letter from inside his shirt and hands it to Benson while he continues to speak.*) I wasn't aware that certain pieces of furniture had such uses, and I certainly was not aware that the magistrate was so flexible. Mind you, I could tell that this woman was.

11

Benson:	My God...(*Reading letter.*)
Leo:	Yes, quite vivid, is it not? Just imagine what his wife would think about it.
Benson:	Well, she might learn a thing or two from it. (*Still reading the letter with a very amused face.*)
Leo:	Yes, in more ways than one, eh? (*Looking at Benson with a hinting gaze.*)
Benson:	(*Meets his gaze and folds up the letter.*) Ah, I see, I need a drink. (*Goes back to the table and grabs the bottle of wine.*)
Leo:	It seems you are no longer bored.
Benson:	Certainly not. So you intend to expose him.
Leo:	If he doesn't pay a price. (*Taking the wine and taking a swig himself.*)
Benson:	I take it you have some form of a plan and, as per usual, you will require my assistance.
Leo:	Well, one must be sober to create a plan, which leaves you right out. So to answer your question, yes. I have a plan, and it will require your assistance. Best of all, unlike some of our schemes in the past, this one will work.
Benson:	So what is it that you will require of me?
Leo:	Yes well, I certainly cannot have the magistrate think I am involved with blackmailing him, or the situation at work could get rather awkward and may in fact become hazardous to my health. Therefore, it will be you blackmailing him, so to speak.
Benson:	I follow. I think. No, not at all. Please elaborate.
Leo:	Tomorrow I will arrive at the law office early. I will leave a note from the blackmailer, you, which will tell him that you have a letter, which will prove he is having an affair. The letter will instruct him to have money ready to pay you at midday when you will arrive at the office, disguised, of course, then you will collect the money and give the letter to the magistrate, and we will meet here at this pub and split the money. I will arrive after the magistrate in

the morning and return the costume, ensuring that I look innocent and possess no knowledge of the events transpiring. You can ask for any sum you choose, and we will split it. Just make it, big because we know he will pay it. He has a lot to lose, including his wife, wealth as well as position, rank and reputation.

Benson: I see, that is not a half bad plan.

Leo: I know.

Benson: It is a night for celebration, and I concur with you; this scheme does seem as though it should work.

Leo: Yes, so let us go and seek some more merriment among our class, for by tomorrow night we will be living in a higher estate.

The two men leave the pub with their masks in their hand and walk across center stage as the light follows them from stage left to exit on stage right. They pass a pile of crates, boxes and random rigging and nets. From behind the pile, as they pass by and exit, Arthur "Art" Checker the pirate slowly rises with his pistol in hand.

Art: There be magistrate Rawlings, with the blue jester mask as promised. Laugh while you can ,you great cheating landlubber! For on the morrow you'll be having a meeting with my pistol, and you will be judged, Har. (*The gun accidentally goes off in the air as he holds it.*) Blast! I hope that does not happen tomorrow before I acquire what I need from that scurvy swine. Now to reload. (*Checks his pouch for musket balls.*) Arrrrrr, most embarrassing, out of musket balls.

Scene II

Stage is set with a couple of desks and a bookshelf. There are numerous papers and charts, books all strewn over the office, and ink wells and quills on the desk. The magistrate comes on from stage right and is dressed in his typical black robes and his wig. He is carrying some papers and seems to be in a generally solemn and serious mood. He goes over to his desk and picks up a note he sees laying on top of it.

Rankin: A letter addressed to me. What bothersome business do I have to attend to now? (*Opens the letter and begins to read, clearly growing more displeased as he does so.*) Blackmail me? Blackmail me?!

How did this man get his hands on a letter which proves my infidelity? Not that I can deny it, but who can blame me? My wife is hideous but necessary, so this situation will not do! Not to mention I am a magistrate. I cannot appear to mixed up in scandalous or illegal affairs; they must remain secret! I shall have to take all of this out on my clerk, Leonard Butterfield. So help me if my costume I lent him is not returned in proper order, I'll hang him from my gallows myself! No, I must be calm. I can not appear as though anything is wrong. I must go and collect my money and be ready for this crook's visit at midday. (*Leo enters, holding the borrowed costume and mask, and the magistrate quickly hides away the letter.*) Good morning, Mr. Butterfield. Did you have an enjoyable New Year's?

Leo: I did indeed, Magistrate Rawlings. Thank you very much for allowing me the use of your costume last night. You could say it proved to be the life of the party. (*Handing it back.*)

Rankin: Very good.

Leo: If I might inquire, Sir, where was it that you were off to last night that kept you from the festivities?

Rankin: Business, what else.

Leo: Does your wife get upset about you being out so often?

Rankin: What?! (*Clearly his mind still on the blackmail letter.*)

Leo: I just mean given that you are always so busy, you know how women can be such a bother.

Rankin: Yes, indeed they can be. (*He turns to fiddle with his bookshelf.*)

Leo: (*To himself.*) Wonderful, I can tell he's flustered. He must have read the letter. I could leave this alone, but I think I want to have some fun. Not everyday I can make Rankin Rawlings sweat. (*To Rawlings.*) I must say, there were some incredible beauties out and about last night.

Rawlings: How's that?

Leo: Well, certainly you can appreciate the look of a beautiful woman.

Rawlings: Indeed. After all, look at my wife.

Leo:	Oh yes, very fetching. But a man like you, among all those high society damsels, some days your view must be very nice.

Rawlings:	You forget your place, Mr. Butterfield. You are my clerk, not my equal! Do not speak so familiarly with me.

Leo:	Begging your pardon, Sir. I mean no offence, just in too chipper of a mood after the festivities. Actually, I met this one girl last night. Her name was Anne. She was quite charming, and I do believe I will write her today. Did you and your wife ever do that, ever write letters to each other?

Rawlings:	No, never. I do not like to write letters, I do not like to read letters. Words are tedious! I have to step out, Butterfield. Look after the office until I return, and do not touch anything on my desk.

Leo:	Very well, Sir.

Rawlings quickly gathers a few paper, tucks them under his arm, hurries out of the office, and exits stage right. As soon as he gets offstage Leo begins howling with laughter)

Leo:	That went brilliantly. I am certain he is on his way to go and collect the money to pay Benson when he arrives. This will be a fantastic day. (*As Leo is being amused by himself and his exploits, Arthur Checker enters onto the stage from stage right and is holding his gun. When Leo looks up, he is startled to see the pirate standing in front of him and pointing a pistol directly at him.*) Not often one of you freely walks into our office. Normally your kind is dragged.

Art:	Aye! But not today, Magistrate Rawlings. I am here for two reasons. One is to reacquire that which you have taken from me, or from my brother to be more precise. Secondly is to dispense a little justice upon you, such as you like to freely deliver to whomever you choose.

Leo:	I assume by that you mean to kill Magistrate Rawlings, but, from where I am standing, Sir, you have two problems. One, your pistol is not cocked, and two, I am not Magistrate Rawlings.

Art:	Aye, wait, what?! (*Confused.*)

Leo:	Yes, I am Leonard Butterfield, Leo for short, and I am the law clerk of magistrate Rawlings, who has stepped out. Shall I leave him a message, something to the effect of "rot and die you scurvy

scum"?

Art:	You must be lying, I saw you last night in the blue jester costume. I was specifically told that the magistrate always wears that costume on New Year's, and my sources are very reliable.
Leo:	I am sure, with you being a pirate and all, but I borrowed the magistrate's costume last night. In fact, he leant it to me. So, now you know who I am, but I am curious who you are.
Art:	I am Arthur Checker, fearsome pirate, but you can call me Arrrrrrrrrrt for short.
Leo:	Right. Would you mind putting the gun down now?
Art:	Aye. (*Puts the gun back in his belt.*) This has not been one of my finest pirating moments.
Leo:	No doubt. You mentioned something about an item you wish to regain from the magistrate. What is that about?
Art:	'Tis a treasure map.
Leo:	Of course, you are a pirate. And you say Rawlings has it?
Art:	Arrr, he must. He stole it from me brother a year ago or so, the last letter from my brother. He sent it shortly before Magistrate Rawlings had him hung, but not before he stole the treasure map from my brother.
Leo:	Incredible.
Art:	What is?
Leo:	Oh, it is just inspiring to me how noble Magistrate Rawlings appears and then to learn just how rotten he truly is. It's something to aspire to. So, you have never seen Magistrate Rawlings?
Art:	No. After my brother sent his last letter I was determined to find him, though, both to avenge my brother and to get back the map which, due to my brother's untimely passing, means all the treasure will be mine.
Leo:	Well, Art, I have a proposal for you of a daring nature.

Art: Aye, go on.

Leo: While the magistrate is out, why not search the office? Between the two of us we should find the map and, when we do, we can use it and split the treasure.

Art: You've a deal. (*Shakes Leo's hand.*)

            The two begin to start searching the office, being careful to replace whatever they move where they found it. The magistrate then appears coming back on from stage right, and behind him is a man clothed in a masquerade costume and mask, Benson. Leo catches sight of this and quickly gets the pirate and himself to hide behind the bookshelf as the other two reach the desks.

Rawlings: Butterfield is not even in the office for me to send him home. What an unreliable and useless little sot! And you, Sir, do not realize the grave mistake you are making in blackmailing me. I am a powerful man and, when I discover who you are, I promise I will have you swinging by the next day.

Benson: Ha, no doubt but that is why I am disguised. (*Clearly he is again intoxicated.*) Now, I suggest you hand over the sum I have requested, and I will give you the letter, and we can happily part ways. (*While these two are talking, both Art and Leo are listening*)

Rawlings: You have made no demand for a sum yet.

Benson: Right! Indeed. Then I shall do that. (*Leo hangs his head.*) I think that one thousand pounds is a nice round number.

Rawlings: One Thousand pounds!

Benson: Well, can you really place a price on marital bliss and the happy secure life you have?

Rawlings: You are going to pay.

Benson: Actually, I think you are.

Rawlings: Are what?

Benson: Precisely!

Rawlings: What?

Benson: Going to pay.

Rawlings: Who is?

Benson: Both of us, apparently.

Rawlings: Are you drunk?

Benson: Always. One thousand pounds, now.

Rawlings: Indeed. I'll pay you now and hang you later. (*He pulls out a bag of gold and hands it to him.*) There is a thousand pounds in there. Now give me the letter.

Benson: Happily. It was a charming read. (*Benson puts the bag of gold in one pocket and produces the letter from another and hands it to the magistrate.*) Good day, Sir. (*Benson turns and exits stage right.*)

Rawlings: A fortune! This cost me a fortune. (*Stuffing the letter in his pocket. Art now tries to move out from behind the bookshelf.*)

Leo: (*Holding him back.*) Wait! What are you doing?

Art: He's on his own. Now is my chance to get the map and revenge.

Leo: Wait. Your gun is still not cocked.

Art: No matter, I am out of musket balls any way.

Leo: Then that may be even more reason to be patient. Bloody pirates.

Rawlings: (*Moving to his desk.*) Although this is not an ideal situation, my lost wealth can be recovered. I have a plan for that. (*Opens up a box with a key which was in his desk and pulls out the map.*) An advantage to dealing with pirates is that their booty can quite quickly become your own. I shall simply charter a ship and find this treasure for myself. Perhaps it was excessive, hanging the man after robbing him of his treasure map, but better safe than sorry. Enough plotting. (*Putting the map away.*) For now, I need to destroy this letter permanently and, when I see Butterfield, I am going to enjoy taking all of my frustrations out on him! (*Rawlings gets up and grabs a few more papers and exits stage right. Leo and Art come out from behind the bookshelf.*)

Leo: There, you see what I told you. Now we know the location of the map, and now you can seek your revenge on Rawlings when you have the proper tools, such as the musket balls to do so. (*Motioning to where the magistrate hides the box with the map in the desk.*) Shall we?

Art: Aye, 'bout time I reclaimed what is mine.

Leo: How did you come by this map? (*Grabbing the box out of the desk.*)

Art: 'Twas on a boat. My ship jumped aboard another pirate vessel, and my brother, Vincent, and I found it searching the bodies of the dead.

Leo: Who is Vincent?

Art: He was another member of our crew. When the three of us found the map it was a matter of simple math. Splitting a treasure two ways means more than splitting it three ways. So through a process of elimination...

Leo: (*Cutting in.*) Vincent not being family.

Art: No, him being the only one wearing no clothing which was red in colour, he was selected to die, and we ran him through. My brother and I then returned to the rest of the crew and told them we had found nothing, and that Vincent had tripped and fallen upon his own sword.

Leo: Very good. (*Clearly stupefied by Art.*) And how was your brother captured?

Art: Arrrr, Willie explained that in the final letter he wrote. He made a big mistake and confused one of the nobility's houses for a brothel. I think the lady of the house was most surprised, but her daughter didn't seem too troubled.

Leo: Those kind of young ladies are the best, very...um...eager to please. (*He removes the map from the box and, when he looks up, he sees Art pointing his pistol at him.*) What exactly is it that you're doing?

Art: I am taking the map.

Leo: Therefore welching on our deal.

Art:	Aye, but I am a pirate, so it was foolish to expect anything different from me.
Leo:	You forget, I am fully aware that your pistol is not loaded.
Art:	(*Thinking for a moment.*) 'Tis true. Good thing I carry this. (*Pulls out a dagger.*)
Leo:	I see. Well, that does complicate things. (*Moving to evade Art.*) But I have no intention of giving it up easily.
Art:	Give it here! (*Grabbing onto the map that Leo is still holding. He swings his dagger a few times, and Leo avoids getting hit by the blade while still holding onto the map. After a small comedic struggle, the map ends up getting ripped in half, and both of the men have a piece*) I will find ye soon and, when I do, I expect to take the whole map for myself! (*Exits stage right.*)
Leo:	(*Calling after him.*) Well, you had better get some ammunition first!

Scene III

The stage is once again set to resemble the pub in the center of the stage. There is the background noise of moving glasses and people laughing. Benson is sitting at the table and has a bottle of wine and a couple of glasses with him. He is sitting on the stage left side of the table, and Leo enters from stage right into the pub.

Leo:	My dear Benson Belch, I am quite happy to see you. It has been a rather exasperating day.
Benson:	Indeed, no doubt. I am certain working with Rawlings today was an absolute treat, given his disposition. I have just the cure for you, though. (*Holds out the bottle of wine.*)
Leo:	I believe I will. (*Drinks some.*) So, how much did you take from our friend the magistrate today?
Benson:	Well, you will indeed be needing to drink as much as you can, as I am afraid the news on that subject is not as happy as you may be seeking to find it.

Leo:	Really? (*Sitting down.*)
Benson:	Yes. I must confess I, as per usual, had indulged my love of wine before I went to visit Rawlings at midday. I even accosted him on the street in my disguise, which was not more than my masquerade costume, and escorted him back to the office. There, in my stupor, I only thought to weasel out of him two hundred pounds. So, split two ways, that is one hundred each. A far better cry than nothing, but not as much as you may have hoped for.
Leo:	(*To Benson.*) I see. That is very surprising.
Benson:	How do you mean?
Leo:	(*Rising.*) Well, I find it interesting that there is only a mere one hundred pounds for me, as I happened to be hiding in the office when you asked the magistrate for one thousand pounds!
Benson:	Really, you were present. Hmmmm that I had not expected.
Leo:	No doubt, you rat! I wonder as to where the other nine hundred pounds will make its home, if I am only receive one hundred. I am going to propose an educated guess that they will rest with you.
Benson:	Not true. I expected they would rest with the owner of this pub, given that they would be spent primarily on wine.
Leo:	Swine! (*Leaps across the table onto Benson and is wrestling him to the ground when Art enters into the pub from stage left and makes his way behind Leo. He puts the pistol to the back of Leo's head, and Leo freezes while Benson looks up with surprise and confusion.*)
Art:	I decided to do as you instructed and got some more musket balls. Now hand over the other half of me map.
Leo:	What very inconvenient timing.
Benson:	Who is this?
Leo: B	enson Belch, meet Arthur Checker, he is a pirate.
Benson:	Obviously.

Art: Call me Arrrrrrrrrt for short.

Leo: I have no intention of giving you the other half of the map, as I
            fully believe you are bluffing about acquiring musket balls. (*Art
            fires a shot up into the air.*) Fair enough.

Benson: What is this map which he is speaking about?

Art: 'Tis a map me and my brother found.

Leo: On a dead man.

Art: Aye, leads to a treasure which I aim to collect, so hand over the
            map.

Leo: (*Producing his half of the map.*) Well, here it is, but you will
            never get your hands on it.

Art: I think I will. (*Motioning with his pistol.*)

Leo: Oh, I am aware you have the gun, but I am also aware that you
            just fired, thus you are once again unarmed.

Art: Well....Aye, Arrrrrr....Blast!

Leo: Quite. You see, we could have avoided any difficulty if you were
            just willing to split the treasure with me.

Benson: Ah ha!

Leo: What are you on about?

Benson: You were going to make a deal with this pirate and get yourself a
            heap of treasure and cut out your best friend, me, to get a larger
            cut for yourself!

Art: It seems I am rubbing off on you. 'Tis but simple math. Treasure
            split between two means more than treasure split between three.
            (*Grabs the other half of the map from Leo.*) Yaaarrrr. Tis all
            mine now!

Leo: (*Grabbing onto one side of the half.*) I think not. (*The two begin
            to hold a tug of war over the piece while Benson quickly picks
            Art's pocket and produces the other half of the map.*)

22

Benson:	Well, I've no intention of sitting idly by when there is treasure to be had.
Art:	(*Grabbing hold of the other side of the half that Benson is holding.*) You best give that back if ye value your life.
Benson:	Truly, I don't think it is worth all that much.

All three of the men begin to struggle over the pieces and eventually both halves rip in half and produce four quarters. Two are in the possession of Art, one rests with Leo, and one with Benson

Art:	(*Leaving from the pub.*) We shall meet again, and next time I will not be alone. The map will be mine! (*He exits stage right, leaving Leo and Benson on their own, staring at one and other as they hold onto their quarters.*)
Leo:	Well, this is proving to be a most productive day.
Benson:	(*Returns to the table and picks up his bottle of wine.*) I'll drink to that.
Leo:	You know, if we put the two quarters together that we both possess, we are half way to our goal.
Benson:	While I agree, I think you would be hard pressed to convince Art to join in and split the treasure three ways. Furthermore, why should I trust you?
Leo:	Perhaps you shouldn't, but think of the treasure.
Benson:	It outweighs the risk, but I still say that Art will never be convinced.
Leo:	I don't believe the goal should be to convince him, but instead simply take the pieces from him and then split the treasure just between us. Two ways does mean more than three.
Benson:	I'll drink to that as well. (*Drinks.*) But what about his threats?
Leo:	He has threatened me twice now. I have been fine on both occasions, more or less. Besides, I have a plan, and it is good.
Benson:	I have my doubts about that.
Leo:	My last plan worked quite well, I think. Look, I have a good sus-

picion as to what his next move will be, and I have a way that we can outsmart Art.

Benson: Well, that particular venture doesn't seem like it would be too difficult.

Leo: Well, if you can pick up on his stupidity, then clearly he is a very sad case.

Benson: Right. So what is this plan?

Leo: Sit down, my good Sir. (*Motioning to the table.*) Pour a drink and listen to what I have to tell you, oh, and also do give me money you collected from our friend the magistrate. You can trust me. (*The two sit down and lean in close and begin to plot.*)

ACT II

Scene I

The stage is set to the Magistrate's office. The Magistrate is sitting at his desk, going over some papers, and Leo enters onto stage and makes his way over to his desk. As soon as the magistrate sees him, he gets up and moves over to him.

Rawlings: Mr. Butterfield, I wonder if I might have a word with you.

Leo: (*Turning to face him.*) Yes Sir, of course. What about?

Rawlings: Just a few small matters.

Art: (*Entering from stage right.*) Aye, just a few small matters.

Leo: (*Clearly afraid now.*) Oh....

Rawlings: Yes, my dear Leo, we need to have a chat. A chat about theft of property, blackmail and impersonating me! You have been busy with your little friend, haven't you? Well now your misadventures stop, at the gallows. However, before that happens, there are a few small matters we need to clear up.

Leo: I suppose an apology wouldn't work to satisfy everything and grant me a pardon?

24

Rawlings: Not even close. I must commend you; your schemes were not half bad. You just picked the wrong target. Now, on that note, there are a few items I need to collect from you. My thousand pounds, the piece of the treasure map you have in your possession, and the name and location of your friend.

Leo: Right. If I might, how did you figure all of this out?

Rawlings: I would have thought that obvious. Your friend, Arthur Checker over here, turned you in. In exchange, we are working together to recover the pieces of the map and split the treasure, once it is found.

Art: Aye, I told you the next time we met I would have friends.

Leo: Odd choice in friends, the man that killed your brother. You yourself were planning to kill him only yesterday.

Art: 'Tis true. I suppose his friendship is a matter of connivance, really.

Rawlings: Now, hand over my money and the map piece. (*Holding out his hand.*)

Leo: (*Reluctantly hands over the piece of map and the bag of the Magistrate's money.*) Well, this is far from how I wanted things to work out.

Rawlings: No doubt, but then the world doesn't have happy endings for the likes of the poor and miserable urchins like you. Oh, and this may seem like a moot point, since I intend to hang you tomorrow, but you are fired.

Art: We still need the final piece of the map.

Rawlings: I am fully aware of that. Now Leo, I think it is time you took us to your friend so we can collect what he owes us. What is his name?

Leo: If you want I could just fetch it from him myself. I dragged him into this, and he doesn't need to be punished because of me.

Rawlings: Don't bother trying to be noble now. It just doesn't suit you. Hand him over to us, and he can swing next to you, true friends and partners in crime.

Leo: His name is Benson Belch.

Rawlings: Yes, that name does suit him from my encounter with him. I promised him he'd hang for blackmailing me, and now I will make good on my promise. Come, Leo, lead us on to where he might be. (*Rawlings leaves the office with Leo coming out after him, being trailed by Art.*)

Scene II

The stage is set with three different set pieces. Stage left is set to the pub and inside Benson is sitting on the stage right of the table with a bottle of wine. Centre stage is clear and meant to portray the outside of the pub. Stage right is set to be the deck of a small ship, with the mast visible and a few crates and some rigging and nets. Leo, Rawlings and Art all enter the pub from stage left. Leo enters first.

Benson: Leo, come have drink with me, I ... (*Stops speaking upon seeing Rawlings and Art enter.*) You brought friends.

Rawlings: (*Moving over to Benson.*) So here is the face behind the mask that blackmailed me. You drunken fool, I told you that I would hang you and I shall, but first I will be needing the final piece of the map, which I know is in your possession. (*While the magistrate is speaking, Benson quickly picks the magistrate's pocket, hides the map pieces in his own pocket, and replaces them with different pieces.*) Hand it over now, and I promise you a slow and relatively painless death.

Benson: With such a wonderful offer, how can I refuse? (*He reaches into his pocket and pulls out another map piece.*) You have to admit, for a drunk, I made quite the fool out of you.

Rawlings: (*Pulls out all the map pieces to quickly glance and see that they fit together.*) Indeed. Both of you did and, believe me, you will suffer for it. Though I am curious now that you mention it, how did the two of you get your hands on that letter from my mistress?

Leo: You recall when you leant me your costume on New Year's.

Rawlings: Yes.

Leo: Well, I did attend a party, but not my regular one. Seeing as how I looked like you in the costume that you wear every year, I decided to go to the Earl of Chutney's ball. There your mistress came to me, believing me to be you behind your mask. She put the letter into my hands and then dashed off. I simply decided to take advantage of the situation.

Rawlings: I see. Well, at least I know how to avoid this from happening again. Arthur, do accompany me outside for a moment.

Art: Aye.

Rawlings: Now, do not run off anywhere gentlemen. I will be very disappointed if I don't get to see the two of you swing. (*Both men gulp as Rawlings and Art step to centre stage. The lights go up on them and go down on the pub set. Leo and Benson slip offstage while stage left is in the dark.*)

Art: So, when shall we charter a boat to go after our treasure?

Rawlings: Well, I plan to charter a boat in the near future. You, however, have a different future ahead of you. (*He produces some manacles from his robe and slaps them onto Art.*)

Art: Arrr, what is this?!

Rawlings: What do you think? You are a pirate. You are under arrest. It simply wouldn't due to have a magistrate such as myself associating with a criminal such as you. It wouldn't be proper. I do, however, have every intention of retrieving the treasure on my own after I am hailed for hanging yet another pirate. (*Pulling out the map.*) Now, let me see where exactly I must plan to travel too. (*Begins to look more intently at the map.*) No!

Art: What? (*Rawlings holds the map in front of Art, who reads it.*) Better luck next time.

Rawlings: They switched the map but when, how!

Art: You might be wanting to check the bag of money he gave you as well. (*Rawlings reacts in a panic and grabs the bag. He opens it up and pulls out some polished stone from inside it into his hand.*)

Rawlings: Rocks! The switched the Pounds for rocks! And I left them unwatched. Oh no. (*Rawlings runs back onto stage left, and the lights come up on the empty pub set*) No, no, no!

The lights go down on Art and Rawlings and come up on stage right, where Benson and Leo are sitting on the ship's deck with a bottle of wine and toasting with two glasses.

Leo: Fantastic. I must say, that played out even better than I thought it would.

Benson: I'll drink to that. (*Drinks.*)

Leo: How I would have loved to see their faces, especially Magistrate Rawlings when he reads the map and looks at his pounds. Excellent work, by the way, of switching the map pieces.

Benson: Thank you. Though I must commend you on your plan, utterly brilliant.

Leo: Well, I based it on the principle that started our whole situation. When I wore the Magistrate's costume on New Year's, everyone assumed that I was him. They judged everything on the outward appearance, so it stood to reason both Art and Rawlings would do the same. The Magistrate's bag filled with rocks to the proper amount did so effectively appear to be full of his pounds.

Benson: The pounds which purchased this boat.

Leo: Indeed. It wasn't to hard to make the fake map pieces. Just take a piece of paper, crease it, fold it and stain it with tea and it looks like the tattered and old treasure map. At quick glance the pieces we made all fit together and looked similar to the map but with further exploration the two villains will discover naught but a taunting message. It seems people love to take appearance for granted and fail to see so much of what lies beneath the surface. No doubt that is how Magistrate Rawlings has maintained his position and marriage for so long.

Benson: No doubt. Let us see the map, eh. (*Leo passes the pieces to him.*) This should prove to be quite the adventure.

Leo: With us it often does.

Benson: How did you know they would leave us alone so we could escape?

Leo: Well, I knew they were both ruthless and were bound to turn on each other the first chance they could. At some point I figured their scheming would get the better of them and, while trying to get ahead, they would forget about us completely.

Benson: Bloody marvelous! So, what do you expect we will do once we have the treasure? Do you plan to make yourself a magistrate?

Leo: No, I fear I am too honest a man for that position.

Benson: What then?

Leo: What we do best?

Benson: Which is?

Leo: Well, you, my good man, will drink.

Benson: I like the sounds of that. (*Belches.*) And you?

Leo: I, I will scheme.

The two men toast each other, and upbeat classical music begins playing as the lights go down on the whole of the stage

HOT PURSUIT

A note on *Hot Pursuit*

This was a fun production, and the laughs during the rehearsals were as loud and often as from the audience when the production went into full swing. This production was bound to get interesting, due to all of the low comedy and blatant sexual comedy. The posters described the show as "A Midsummer Night's Dream meets American Pie." That was a very fair description. It definitely could not be considered a family-friendly production. The audience that could attend it, however, did enjoy it and found it to be a fun production. The play was an adaptation of *A Midsummer's Night Dream* and was created to run with the Canadian Shakespeare Festival in 07/08. The main note I would like to share on this play is not about the script but primarily about the actual production and our move-in day and opening night.

We had moved into the theatre at 4:30pm. I was running on a tight schedule for the production, as the opening show started at 9pm that very night. So, what did we have to accomplish in that time? We had to build the set, move in all the props, organize the tech and do a tech run. We had to figure out scene changes and let the actors get used to being on the stage. The cast had five members to it: Alicia Savage - Nicole, Jenn Burt - Love, Jessi-Rae Larsen - Shelly, Hayden Arnell - Paul and myself - Mark. The man in charge of our tech was Paul Caughill and, due to people canceling at the last minute, his only tech help was going to be my father after he helped construct the set. I am sure you can tell from the information I have told you, things were not going to go as smooth as I may have hoped.

The first surprise occurred when we entered the theatre to find an orchestra set up on the stage for a concert that was not occurring until the Sunday after my show. So, our first major task became removing that from the stage by hand and by ourselves. It seemed my ambitious timetable was already coming around to bite me in the ass. Sometimes my ambition does have a tendency to do that. The next surprise encounter came during the tech set up, when we discovered that the sound and lights could not be set up next to each other, or strange feedback would come through the speakers when certain lights were turned on. This meant that my father had to set up and run sound from the back of the theatre while Paul ran lights from the front of the house. This left my father without any guidance on the sound except for some hastily scribbled notes, the result of which was that at one point in the play, when the music should have cut out much, much earlier, it did not. This just happened to be the scene where the one actress was dancing topless, and for far longer than ever intended. It was an awkward moment, and I was on my knees practically tearing my hair out as I watched it occur. Ah, memories.

When the curtain went up at 9:00 pm, it was without a tech run or rehearsal on the stage with my cast, and only a verbal explanation of what I wanted done for the scene changes. I ended up being in charge of running the curtain that night, as well, and being the primary set changer, due to the lack of time I had to teach them to my cast. Completely to my cast's credit, though, we put on the show, and the audience enjoyed it. There were some definite flubs, but some lessons have to be learned harder than others. After that experience, I will never have my move-in day and opening night in the same day. I simply will not do it.

Characters

Paul: A typical "guy" who is in love with a not-so-typical girl who is extremely different from him. He's willing to do a lot of crazy things, however, and go out of his comfort zone a lot to win her heart. Of course, needless to say, he's rather awkward at everything he does.

Nicole: An artistic beauty for whom Paul has fallen. She loves poetry and dancing and has a real fun side about her. She is sensitive and often unsure of the situations she is finding herself in when regarding Paul.

Shelly: Shelly is the frustrated girlfriend of Mark who has, thanks to magic, fallen in love with Paul. She is also an unlikely ally to help Paul win over Nicole and is often involved in creating compromising situations.

Mark: Shelly's boyfriend who has become attracted to Paul, thanks to magic. He is a fun guy who likes to dance and is skilled at it. The key thing to remember is that Mark is a straight guy who is pursuing Paul like he would pursue a woman.

Love: The embodiment of love. Uses magic to help Paul in his quest but at the same time makes his life difficult. Love seems to take pleasure in people's happiness and in their pain. A very interesting and confusing character that becomes the living paradox that is love.

Hot Pursuit

ACT I

Scene I

A light comes up on stage showing a sign for a bus stop. Paul is onstage, and Nicole is sitting on a bench listening to music.

Paul: There she is, Nicole, the girl of my dreams. And what dreams she has inspired! Unfortunately, I'll never have anything but my dreams, because she's way out of my league. She's one of those really artsy girls and, as far as I'm concerned, the playboy center-fold is art in its highest form, and poetry is good for wiping your ass. But everyday she comes and waits for the bus, and everyday I come and watch. (*Pause.*) No, I'm not a stalker. I'm just observing her, like a predator watching its pray. Okay, bad example, but you get the idea. I can't help it, I'm in love. To have her be my girl would make me the happiest man on Earth. (*There is the sound of a bus, and Nicole gets up and leaves.*) I hate to see her go, but I love to watch her leave. Hey, it's just another observation. (*Love enters onstage.*)

Love: I've been doing a little observing of my own, and I've observed that you clearly want to get with that girl.

Paul: Who are you?

Love: I'm love, or at least the one in charge of or overseeing it. Now, obviously you think that girl is fabulous.

Paul: Yeah, but way out of my league.

Love: Oh most definitely, yes.

Paul: So, if you're in charge of love, aren't you supposed to support me?

Love: I'm love, not the happy hand holding circle. I'm not here for support. I'm here to help love happen. If you had a chance, I wouldn't be here to help you, and you need help.

Paul: So, you are like cupid?

Love:	Do I look like a little baby with a bow and arrow and wings?
Paul:	Well...
Love:	Don't answer that. Geez, you're stupid. No, I am not cupid. I'm here to help.
Paul:	Why?
Love:	Because I'm Love.
Paul:	We're not getting very far.
Love:	Look, I'm helping you because the more love around the world the better life is for me. So, I'll help you get your love to better me.
Paul:	A self-serving love.
Love:	Like there's any other.
Paul:	So, how are you going to help me?
Love:	First of all, maybe try talking to the girl. All this watching is a little creepy. No, it's really creepy.
Paul:	Talk, yeah, that doesn't go so well with me. Talking, dating, relationships, I'm bad at it.
Love:	Of course, you're a man. But I have something that will tip the odds. (*Love produces the magic kit.*) Inside this kit there are several magic items that may be helpful in your pursuit.
Paul:	Like what?
Love:	Well, primarily there is a love potion. You drink half, get your girl to drink the other, and boom! Instant love.
Paul:	Seriously?!
Love:	You'll be hopping on one foot and doing the bad thing in no time.
Paul:	What?
Love:	Sex, you'll be getting a lot of it.

Paul:	Yes.
Love:	(*Quietly.*) No more Kleenex and Palmolive for you.
Paul:	What?
Love:	Nothing. So you want the package?
Paul:	Yes!
Love:	Okay, just remember, I have to get a new love out of this, or I will curse you in this field.
Paul:	I've been pretty cursed so far.
Love:	You a eunuch yet?
Paul:	No.
Love:	Then you have something to lose. See ya. (*Love exits.*)
Paul:	Holy shit. This is crazy. (*Tears open the package and grabs the love potion.*) Nice, instant sex in a bottle. (*He downs half the bottle.*) I have to find Nicole. This is gonna be a good day. Funny, you'd think I would feel bad about not gaining her love. But I'm still gonna get laid. Let's see, labour and true love on one hand or fake love, no work and instant sex. Hell, the romantic period died long ago, I'm a man of the 21st century. Fake love and free sex works for me. (*Exits.*)
Love:	(*Re-enters.*) Either that boy is going to fuck things up horribly, or his right hand is going to get lonely.

Scene II

Nicole is sitting with Mark in a coffee shop. They are both on stools at the coffee bar. Mark has a cup of coffee, and Nicole is working on some notes. There is the sound of voices and bustle in the coffee shop.

Nicole:	Our English class is great.
Mark:	Right. Well, I guess you enjoy poetry and Shakespeare. Personally, I despise it.

Nicole:	Why do you study it?
Mark:	Because I'm good at it.
Nicole:	How can you be good at something you hate?
Mark:	Well, I talk with my girlfriend all the time.
Nicole:	What happens when she asks you deep questions?
Mark:	Same thing when we're asked deep questions in English: I bullshit. Hey, I have to run for a couple minutes, can you watch my coffee?
Nicole:	Sure, Mark.
Mark:	Thanks (*He exits, and Paul enters with the love potion.*)
Paul:	There she is, and there is her coffee. Now I just need a chance to put the potion in it.
	Nicole gets a call on her cell phone. She turns around and takes the call.
Nicole:	Hello, yeah, I'm still coming by.
	Paul sneaks up and dumps the potion in her coffee and then steps back to watch.
Nicole:	Okay, see you later.
	Mark comes back in, grabs the coffee and downs it.
Mark:	Wow, that's interesting.
Nicole:	What?
Mark:	I feel kind of funny. Did you do something to it?
Nicole:	No.
Mark:	For some reason, I have a name on my mind, Paul. Oh Paul, the sexy hunk of a man I have to get my hands on.
Nicole:	What?!

Paul:	Oh shit.
Mark:	I want to ride him.
Nicole:	Mark, you have a girlfriend, don't you?
Mark:	That is the past, before Paul.
Nicole:	I…uhhhh.
Mark:	I have to find him.
Paul:	I have to get lost. (*He exits.*)
Mark:	(*Beginning to leave.*) Paul is gonna be mine.
Nicole:	Mark, I think I should come with you. Something is wrong.
Mark:	No, my love is giving me wings, and I have to fly.
Nicole:	What does this Paul look like?
Mark:	I don't know, but when I see him, I know I'll like him. (*Exits.*)
Nicole:	Whatever drug he went and did when he left, I need to get some. (*Nicole leaves, and Paul comes into the coffee shop alone.*)
Paul:	* That did not go as planned. (*Shelly enters.*)
Shelly:	Hey, you okay? You look a little stressed.
Paul:	That's one way of putting it.
Shelly:	Want to talk about it? Maybe I can help.
Paul:	I highly doubt it.
Shelly:	Okay. I'll just leave you alone. (*She sits down on a stool. Mark enters, and she stands*) Mark, honey!
Mark:	Paul! (*Pushes past Shelly. He goes to Paul, spins him around and goes to kiss him, and Paul ducks out of the way.*)
Shelly:	Hello, your girlfriend, Shelly.
Mark:	*I'm sorry, Paul, too forward. I'll move slower, baby. "You are so*

41

beautiful, to me".

Paul: Beautiful? Ripped maybe, sexy maybe, but beautiful?

Mark: Okay, you're cute, and I just want to hold you.

Paul: Oh God!

Shelly: (*Getting between Paul and Mark.*) Hold on. Are you telling me you are leaving me for him? But you're straight.

Mark: I know, but this is burning love.

Shelly: It's ridiculous bullshit! What the hell have you done to him?

Paul: Nothing.

Mark: Oh, you've done something; you've turned me on like nobody ever has before.

Shelly: Hey, I dressed up like a cheerleader for you.

Mark: But Paul's the only one who can make fireworks with me.

Paul: Hell no! There will be no fireworks making or anything else. I'm outta here.

Mark: Wait, we'll have ice cream. (*Pulling out his wallet.*) I have a condom.

Paul: Oh, fuck me.

Mark: Gladly!

Paul: Ahhhh! (*Runs offstage.*)

Shelly: (*Stopping Mark from pursuing him.*) Wait. You are going nowhere. I am taking you home. (*She pushes Mark offstage.*)

Mark: Farewell, Paul. Perhaps I'll get to lay my eyes on your fine ass tomorrow.

Shelly: (*Quietly to the audience.*) Oh no you won't, not when I'm done with him.

Scene III

Paul is sitting in his residence room, desperately digging through his magic kit.

Paul: Where's an antidote, come on! This is not good.

There is a knock at Paul's door, and he goes up against the wall, afraid.

Paul: Who is it?

Shelly: It's Shelly. Open the damn door.

Paul: (*Opening the door just a bit.*) Yes...

Shelly: (*Kicks in the door.*) Okay, what the fuck did you do to Mark? The night before he was all over me, last night he was all over me, and tonight he won't shut up about you. Why! He is not gay, and clearly neither are you. So what is going on?

Paul: Okay, you want the truth?

Shelly: Yes.

Paul: I don't think you're going to believe it.

Shelly: Try me.

Paul: It was a love potion.

Shelly: Right...

Paul: No, I'm serious. I gave him a love potion. Well, not on purpose, but it ended up getting to him.

Shelly: You expect me to believe that.

Paul: And you think your straight boyfriend, falling for a guy who is a total stranger and runs away from him is a rational explanation.

Shelly: Well...

Paul: Look, I got this kit of magic from Love.

Shelly:	Love?
Paul:	Yes. Look, you want answers, then shut-up and let me give them to you.
Shelly:	That's rude.
Paul:	You kicked in my door.
Shelly:	You stole my boyfriend.
Paul:	Can I just tell the damn story?
Shelly:	Fine! So Love gives you some sort of magic kit.
Paul:	Yeah, items that are good for a one-time use to help me go after Nicole.
Shelly:	Nicole?
Paul:	Yes, the girl I like.
Shelly:	Have you ever spoken to her?
Paul:	No.
Shelly:	There's a common theme of love among strangers with you.
Paul:	Will you let me finish? So, in the kit is a love potion. Here's the bottle (*Pulls it out.*) If I drink half and make someone else drink half, they'll fall in love with me. So, I put the potion in her drink, well, what I assumed to be her drink. It ended up being Mark's, and now we have the situation we're in the middle of.
Shelly:	That is 100% Grade A bullshit.
	Love enters.
Love:	Normally I'd have to agree with you, but this time it's the truth.
Shelly:	Who is that?
Paul:	Love.
Shelly:	You're love.

44

Love:	Oh yes.
Shelly:	Okay. Then give him the antidote to the damn love potion you gave him, because it stole my boyfriend from me.
Love:	So, your boyfriend left you for him. I can see why you're upset.
Paul:	Hey!
Love:	And clearly you screwed things up.
Paul:	Yeah, I could use some help.
Love:	I already gave you help.
Paul:	Well, I could use some more.
Shelly:	You can say that again.
Love:	Sorry, you only get one free bit of help. I told you, I get a new love out of the kit, or I curse you in the field. You want more help from me, get me a new love.
Shelly:	And in the meantime, we just let my boyfriend chase after him?
Love:	Should get entertaining.
Paul:	Come on.
Love:	I already explained the rules. You get me a new love, and I'll give you the antidote. Till then, ta-ta. (*Love exits.*)
Paul:	Shit, now what?
Shelly:	Well, that should be obvious, we have to make a new love occur. Who do you know who's single?
Paul:	Me. Who do you know?
Shelly:	No one.
Paul:	Wow, I feel loved.
Shelly:	This Nicole girl you like, she's single, right?

Paul: Yeah.

Shelly: Okay, then the plan is simple. We hook her up with you. Voila! New love.

Paul: If you don't remember, that's how we got into this mess to begin with. I got the potion to accomplish that mission 'cause I can't do it on my own.

Shelly: Well, now you're not on your own. You have me. Plus, there are other items in that magic kit. Let's see what you got and what we can do with it. (*She takes the kit and reads the lid.*) "This is a magic kit direct from Love, all items good for one-time use." Okay let's see what we got. (*As she pulls out an item and the explanation for it.*) Well, there's the explanation of the potion, but we know how that works all too well. And there's "orgasmic chocolate." "The ultimate aphrodisiac, nothing will get you hotter." That may be useful later. What else is there? There is a pen. What does it say about the pen? "The pen of poetics, which, once activated by clicking it three times, will make its speaker possess a lofty speech which will parallel Shakespeare."

Paul: What?

Shelly: That's something you'll clearly be able to use. And then we have, Viagra?

Paul: Let me see that. (*Reads explanation.*) "I don't care what you say, this shit is magic." Okay, that I won't need.

Shelly: (*Under her breath.*) I'm sure it wouldn't hurt.

Paul: Hey, I am fully functioning.

Shelly: Too bad there are zero women to back that statement up.

Paul: I...well...There are some cam girls who could.

Shelly: They don't see you, dumb shit. It's the only way they can keep that job. And on that note of not being seen, this last item looks interesting; "cloak of invisibility."

Paul: What does the explanation say?

Shelly: "Put the cloak on, say the magic phrase. Until the cloak is shed,

46

invisible you'll be." Sounds simple enough.

Paul: Let's see it.

Shelly: (*Pulls out a dress.*) Well, that's interesting.

Paul: That is not a cloak.

Shelly: No, it's not.

Paul: You'll be using that.

Shelly: Oh no! Besides, what do you care? You'll be invisible in it.

Paul: I won't be in it.

Shelly: Well, we need to get some reconnaissance done.

Paul: You're right. You should talk to Nicole, or maybe Mark could. He was talking to her before.

Shelly: Okay, fact number one: the only person Mark wants to talk to is you. Fact number two: we don't have time for talking. We need to know inside information about her fast, so you can sweep her off her feet. So, you are gonna put that dress on, sneak into her room and snoop around to see what you can find.

Paul: Do you have any idea how ridiculous that plan just sounded?

Shelly: I don't care. If it will get my boyfriend to stop starring at your ass sooner, we're doing it. Now go in the closet and put it on.

Paul: This just keeps getting better and better. (*Goes into the closet.*)

Scene IV

Shelly is standing in Paul's room, and Paul is still in the closet.

Paul: So, what's the magic phrase that makes me invisible? 'Cause there is no way I am coming out like this.

Shelly: Oh, come on, Paul, it's about time you come out of the closet.

Paul: (*Opening the door.*) Hey, I'm not gay!

Shelly:	He says, as he's wearing a dress. Maybe you put the potion in Mark's coffee on purpose.
Paul:	Screw you. What's the phrase?
Shelly:	All right, relax. It's "Shazam".
Paul:	All right, here it goes. "Shazam."

Shelly instantly reacts as if Paul has disappeared.

Shelly:	Wow, it worked. I can't see you. Where are you?
Paul:	(*To audience.*) I could have some fun here. (*He starts to sneak up on Shelly, she hears his movement and swings widely, and sacks him.*)
Paul:	Owwwweeeee.
Shelly:	I can't see you, but I can still hear you. Be careful of that when you go to Nicole's room.
Paul:	Right.

He exits through the door and the lights go down on Paul's room and go up on Nicole's. Paul goes to her door, which is open, and sees no one is there.

Paul:	I thought girls were neat. (*He starts going over her desk, reading things as he goes.*) Weekly schedule: tonight, dancing at the club, Friday, dance lessons. The collected works of William Shakespeare. (*Picking up book.*) You could wipe your ass for a year with this. The poetry of Blake. Ha, poetry. I can make poetry. There once was a poet named Blake. He ended up being quite a flake. His work is like…well, the point is it's shit. Okay, I better stick to the pen for poetry. Poetry and I go together as well as President Bush and the English language.

Paul moves, looking over some other items in her room. and picks up some panties on the ground.

Paul:	Well, this looks like a bonus. (*Moves over to her drawer and opens it.*) And we have thongs, and dancing tights, and dancing shoes. So, this girl likes to dance. (*Goes over to her movies.*) Oh my God! When Harry met Sally! I love this movie. (*Looks around to see if*

anyone noticed him.) Oh what do I care? I'm invisible and wearing a dress. What do I really have to hide? (*He puts the movie down, and then Nicole comes into her room and shuts the door.*)

Paul: Oh.

Nicole looks like she thinks she heard something.

Nicole: Must be from another room.

Nicole starts moving around her room, putting her books away, and Paul keeps trying to avoid contact with her or make too much noise.

Nicole: What am I doing tonight? Going to the club. Maybe I should practice my routine for Friday's class a little.

She goes and turns on some music and starts to dance.

Paul: Oh my God, she's flexible.

Nicole: I should probably get changed for tonight.

Nicole continues to dance while stripping. All the while, Paul reacts, and tries to cover the fact with the dress that he's getting an erection. Nicole steps out of her shirt, pants and bra and then puts on an evening dress to go to the club in and shuts off the music. She grabs her cell phone and purse and dials a number.

Nicole: Hey, I'm on my way. (*She exits.*)

Paul: (*Takes a big breath*) Holy Shit. That was great, that was really great.

Paul leaves, and the lights go back up on his room, where Shelly is waiting, and down on Nicole's. He walks in as if in a trance and shuts his door.

Shelly: Paul, is that you?

Paul: Wow.

Shelly: Did you find anything that could help us?

Paul: Oh yeah.

Shelly: What did you see?

Paul: Nothing, I saw nothing of her, I did nothing wrong. My hands did not act immoral.

Shelly: What?

Paul: Never mind.

Shelly: Take the dress off, unless of course you're getting a taste of woman's clothing.

Paul goes back into the closet.

Shelly: So, what did you find out?

Paul: She wears thongs.

Shelly: Wonderful. What else did you find out that's of use?

Paul comes out of the closet, dressed in his usual clothes.

Paul: Well, she likes poetry; she has a lot of it.

Shelly: Well, the pen you have should come in handy then.

Paul: Yeah. And she really likes dancing.

Shelly: Okay.

Paul: It's not okay. I can't dance. That is not a plus for us. Because, trust me, she can dance. Oh boy, can she dance, and shake and (*to Shelly.*) would you mind leaving for a few minutes?

Shelly: Yeah, I would. Whack off later.

Paul: I was just gonna... (*Cut off by Shelly.*)

Shelly: Save it, I have a boyfriend; we've been dating for a few years. I know what you do.

Paul: Wow, women really do know more about men than men know about women.

Shelly: Well, no shit. We have to, it's the only reason you men survive.

50

Besides, your dancing problem can be solved, you just have to learn how.

Paul: Do you know how to dance?

Shelly: No, but Mark does. And, given his current state, I think he'd be more than happy to dance with you.

Paul: Oh no! Fuck that!

Shelly: Hey, you want Nicole? You want Mark to stop chasing you? Then you have to learn, and that means you have to let Mark teach you.

Paul: We're doing it somewhere private.

Shelly: We'll do it at my house.

Paul: And you are not leaving me alone with him.

Shelly: Don't worry. I don't want Mark to do anything under these delusions he's going to regret.

Paul: This is going to be a hell of a night. (*Lights down.*)

Scene V

The lights go up on Shelly's house, and Mark and Shelly are in her living room.

Mark: So, Paul is really coming here tonight?

Shelly: Yes.

Mark: Oh boy. I should have got flowers or chocolates. Is my hair all right? Am I dressed okay? How's my breath? Am I kissable and touchable?

Shelly: Yes, but you will be doing none of that.

Mark: Come on. He's so hot.

Shelly: I am so disturbed.

There is the sound of a door bell.

Shelly: There he is. (*Exits.*)

Mark: (Practicing.) Hey, Paul. Hi, Paul. Hey, sexy. I'm not sure what to go with.

Shelly and Paul enter.

Mark: Wow, Paul. you look great.

Paul: (*To Shelly.*) This is a bad idea.

Mark: I hear you want to learn to dance? Well, I'll teach you some great moves. (*Thrusts crotch out.*)

Paul: (*Looking up.*) Please, no.

Shelly: He needs to learn to dance, but all the dancing will be standing up.

Mark: Okay, so no horizontal Mamba. Maybe we should start with ball-room dancing.

Paul: Right.

Mark: Okay, come over here. Now, I put my hand on your waist, and you put yours on my shoulder, and then…

Shelly: Wait! No, Paul, other way. Mark, he's the guy, he leads. He is learning to dance with a girl.

Mark: All right, just so long as I'm the only guy.

Paul: As odd as it sounds, I truly hope so.

Mark: Okay, reverse the set up, let's begin. You step first. (*They start dancing.*) You should be keeping your back stiffer, like my dick when I'm near you. (*Paul freaks out and backs away.*)

Shelly: Mark, stop. You are dancing, and that's it. With him anyway.

Mark: If I can't have his love, I don't want any.

Shelly: Whatever, start again.

Paul and Mark start again.

Mark:	Twirl me, Paul.
Paul:	No.
Mark:	Twirl me!
Paul:	Fine! (*Twirls him.*)
Mark:	Now I'll twirl you. (*Does so.*) I just had to get another look at that ass of yours.
Paul:	Okay, enough of this.
Mark:	You should probably learn the Tango too.
Shelly:	It couldn't hurt.
Paul:	All right.
Mark:	Okay, this dance is very sensual and needs a lot of close contact.
Paul:	(*Keeps distance and has to lean inward to grasp Mark's hand and waist.*) This is as close as I'm getting.
Mark:	No, closer. (*Reaches out and grabs Paul's ass and pulls him close so that they're touching.*)
Paul:	(*To Shelly.*) Oh God, he is stiff.
Mark:	Okay, let's start.
	Music begins, and the two start to Tango. Mark tips Paul back at the end and goes to kiss him. Shelly pulls him back, Paul falls to the ground, and the music ends.
Shelly:	And that's enough.
Mark:	He'll have to come back and practice.
Paul: H	ell no, I can do that on my own. Damn he's horny!
Shelly:	You have no idea.
Mark:	(*To Paul.*) Well, you could help me out.
Paul:	Goodnight! (*Leaving.*)

Mark:	Yet another sexless night. (*Exits.*)

Shelly:	Hello, I'm right here! Fuck me! Literally, please. I really need it. (*Lights out.*)

ACT II

Scene I

The lights come up on Paul at the bus stop, practicing his dancing alone, looking rather ridiculous and making up moves to the dance that truly do not exist.

Paul:	Well, clearly this is going well. I am never going to get the hang of this. Besides I need a partner to practice partner dancing. I have an idea. I bought this for other purposes, but it will do for this. (*Pulls a package out of a bag.*) Shit. I didn't look when I bought this. It's a man. No wonder the clerk gave me strange looks. Oh well, it will serve my purposes. First time I did this it was with a real guy. I need an air pump; I'll go to the gas station over there. (*Goes off-stage, and there is the sound of an air pump. Paul comes back in, carrying the blown up male blow up doll.*) Okay, now to practice. (*Paul puts his hand on the waist, and the other hand is holding the blow up doll's. He looks down at the blow up doll's dick.*) That's intimidating. (*Shakes his head and starts to Waltz.*) This works better. I should try the Tango. Now, I pull the partner close. (*Blow up doll's dick pushing against Paul.*) Okay, maybe we'll keep our distance. (*Starts dancing. Nicole walks in and stands for a few minutes, watching until Paul notices.*) Oh shit! I… uhhh… I was just practicing, and I…

Nicole:	(*Starts laughing.*) Well, whatever you're doing, I suggest you keep it behind closed doors.

Paul:	I was just practicing some dancing. You see, I need a partner, and I figured the doll would work. I thought I bought a woman one. And…I'm going to give up trying to rationally explain, this because I can't.

Nicole:	You like to dance?

Paul:	Yeah, well, I mean, I'm trying to learn.

54

Nicole:	I love to dance.
Paul:	I know.
Nicole:	What?
Paul:	I'm Paul. (*Holding out his hand.*)
Nicole:	Oh, I'm Nicole. (*Shakes his hand.*)
Paul:	Is there any way we could keep this between us?
Nicole:	It's our secret. (*Going over to the blow up doll.*) Just you, me and Mr. Big.
Paul:	If she likes them big, maybe that Viagra will be useful.
Nicole:	Say, would you like to try practicing with a real partner a little?
Paul:	You mean, you?
Nicole:	Well, unless you prefer his company.
Paul:	No, I'd love to dance with you.
Nicole:	Okay, well then, come over here. Don't be shy.
Paul:	Okay.
Nicole:	Hand on my waist, and take my other hand. Okay, let's try the Waltz first.
	They start dancing, and Paul sort of stumbles over his own feet. Nicole laughs.
Paul:	I told you, I'm just learning.
Nicole:	Everyone has to start somewhere. Try it again. (*They do it fine.*) Good job. Let's try the Tango. First of all, you have to be close. (*Pulls him closer.*) Now let's dance. (*They start to Tango, and Paul tries to dip her. She slips out of his hands onto the ground.*)
Paul:	I'm sorry, my hands are sweaty.
Nicole:	I'm all right. (*Holds out her hand for Paul to help her up, and he*

does.)

Paul: Do you want to try again?

Nicole: No, I should get going, but I'd love to another time. Where do you
           live?

Paul: Elmer Hall.

Nicole: Great, same as me. What room?

Paul: 69.

Nicole: I'll stop by some time. See ya. *(Exits.)*

Paul: Yes! *(Goes to the blow up doll and starts dancing with it again.)*

Scene II

Paul is in his room, looking through the magic kit.

Paul: I might just pull this off. *(Picking up the chocolate.)* "Orgasmic
           Chocolate."

           *There is a knock at Paul's door, and he goes and opens it. Shelly
           walks in, drinking a bottle of pop.*

Shelly: So, have you been practicing your dancing? You need to impress
           Nicole, and quickly. I want Mark back.

Paul: Well, don't you worry. I am making more progress than you think.
           In fact, she wants to go dancing with me.

Shelly: What?! When did you manage that?

Paul: Well, yesterday I was practicing my dancing by the bus stop with a
           blow up doll, and she came across me. She offered to help me and
           stand in as my partner, so we danced a bit, and then she said she
           wanted to do it again and got my room number.

Shelly: You were dancing with a blow up doll?!

Paul: Of the whole story I just told you, the only fact you got was that I
           was dancing with a blow up doll?

Shelly:	Well, it's a little odd.
Paul:	Well, yeah, I thought it wouldn't go over well, especially since it was a male blow up doll.
Shelly:	(*Spitting a mouthful of pop all over Paul.*) I knew it! You are after Mark!
Paul:	Bullshit, I want Nicole. I have seen some of her "features" (*Miming female figure.*) and believe me I want her.
Shelly:	You are horny.
Paul:	Told you I didn't need Viagra.
Shelly:	Oh God. You are nasty.
Paul:	No, I'm a guy. Now this (*Pointing to the pop covered shirt.*) is nasty.
Shelly:	So, a guy dancing with a male blow up doll is what does it for this girl?
Paul:	I doubt it. I don't think my dancing had anything to do with it. My dancing is shit.
Shelly:	Oh, I know that.
	There is a knock at the door.
Paul:	Who is it?
Nicole:	(*From behind the door.*) It's Nicole.
Paul:	Oh shit, you've gotta hide.
Shelly:	What? No, I'm hungry. I have to go get food.
Paul:	No, you have to hide in the closet.
Shelly:	But I'm hungry.
Paul:	Here! (*Handing her the "Orgasmic Chocolate".*) Now get in the closet.

Shelly: (*Looking at the chocolate bar.*) Orgasmic Chocolate.

Paul: Just eat it! (*Stuffs her in the closet and shuts the door and then opens the door for Nicole.*) Hey.

Nicole: Hi. (*Noticing the stain on the shirt.*) Is this a bad time for you?

Paul: No, I was just... uhhh... once again I won't try to rationally explain it.

Nicole: All right, can I come in?

Paul: Sure, sure.

Nicole: Wow, your room is so... well...

Paul: Crappy.

Nicole: Yeah, but so is mine.

Paul: Yes, yes it is.

Nicole: What?! How would you know that?

Paul: Well... I don't but well... ummmm it has to be because...

           Shelly makes an orgasmic sound.

Nicole: What was that?

Paul: Save by the... orgasm?

           Shelly makes another sound.

Nicole: It sounds like it's coming from your closet.

Paul: No.

Shelly: Ewww , ahhhh...yes, oh yes, oh.

Nicole: It sounds like a girl is masturbating in your closet. (*Going to the closet.*)

Paul: (*Stopping her.*) No, no, it's my neighbours. They're just having sex.

Nicole: That doesn't sound like a couple having sex, it...

Shelly: (*Cutting off Nicole.*) Oh yes, yes, yeah, yeah, ohm, owww, eee, eeewww, yes oh yes, oh yeah.

Nicole: Okay, maybe it is sex, but she is definitely faking. How often does this happen?

Paul: Whenever they're in the mood. These walls are like paper, so every once and a while I get an interesting soundtrack.

            Shelly makes very high, squealing orgasmic sounds.

Nicole: Maybe she isn't faking.

Paul: So, why did you come by?

Nicole: I'm going to the club tonight, and I was wondering if you wanted to come dancing.

            Shelly makes more orgasmic noises.

Paul: Sure.

Nicole: I'll come by at eight.

            More orgasmic sounds.

Nicole: I have to go.

Paul: Okay. (*Nicole leaves.*)

            Shelly keeps making orgasmic noises, and Paul goes to the closet and opens it. Shelly is inside, eating the chocolate.

Shelly: Holy shit, this is good chocolate. It's... orgasmic.

Paul: You don't say? The two of us could clearly tell that you were enjoying yourself.

Shelly: Well, I couldn't control myself.

Paul: No shit. (*Grabbing chocolate away.*) You almost screwed everything up. At least we set up our date for tonight before you scared her out of the room.

Shelly:	You have a date with her tonight?
Paul:	Yeah, eight o'clock. She wants to go dancing at one of her clubs.
Shelly:	Excellent, that's excellent. I'll have Mark back in no time.
Paul:	Well, if that's what he has to hear when you guys go at it, I pity him.
Shelly:	Oh, Mark can get me going a lot louder and higher than that.
Paul:	That's great. Thanks for sharing.

Lights fade on Paul's room and come up on the front of the stage, set up to resemble a club. Dance music starts playing, and Paul and Nicole enter onto the stage.

Nicole:	This is going to be fun.
Paul:	Well, you already know I'm not that great of a dancer.
Nicole:	That's why it will be fun. I need a good laugh.
Paul:	Oh, so you want to laugh. Well, laugh at this! (*He tries a few dance steps and slips and falls.*)
Nicole:	Please tell me that was intentional.
Paul:	(*Pause, looking awkward.*) Yes… yes it was. (*Getting up and grabbing his back in pain.*)
Nicole:	So, ready to dance?
Paul:	(*Hunched over and holding his back.*) Oh yeah.
Nicole:	(*Starts dancing*) Well, come a little closer.

Paul walks forward, hunched over, until his head is practically in Nicole's breast.

Nicole:	What are you doing?
Paul:	It's a new style I'm learning.

Nicole:	Right, well, I think you're getting a little too friendly. Now stand up and dance. (*Standing Paul up.*)
Paul:	(*High-pitched.*) Oww! (*Pause.*) Just practicing for when I whip out my Michael Jackson moves.
Nicole:	You're way too stiff when you dance. Loosen up a little.
Paul:	(*Looking incredibly stiff.*) I'm loose.
Nicole:	No, you're not. Here, put your hands on my hips. Can you feel the smoother movement? I'm loose. And bear in mind, we are discussing dancing. (*She puts her hands on him and moves along his body.*) Get more loose, relax. There we go, now you're getting less stiff.
Paul:	(*Looking up.*) In some areas.
Nicole:	What?
Paul:	Nothing at all.
Nicole:	Okay, are you ready to try learning something new?
Paul:	Like what?
Nicole:	Maybe something a little more hip-hop, and a little more risqué?
Paul:	Well I'd... (*Cut off by a cell phone ring.*)
Nicole:	Hold on a moment, I have a call. (*Grabbing her phone.*) Hello... Yes... Oh shit, I completely forgot. No, I'm coming. I'll be there shortly. (*She hangs up the phone.*)
Nicole:	Paul, I'm sorry, I've gotta run.
Paul:	Okay, well then, let's have dinner tomorrow night.
Nicole:	Tomorrow, yeah. I'm free tomorrow. Just come by my room and pick me up.
Paul:	I will.
Nicole:	(*Leaving.*) See you tomorrow. (*She exits.*)
Paul:	Amazing. I've done it!

61

Love enters.

Love: Wow. I have to admit, I was sceptical, even with magic.

Paul: Ah, just the entity I wanted to see. I think it's time for you to re-move that love potion's effects on Mark.

Love: You would think that, but, as almost always, you are wrong yet again.

Paul: What do you mean? I have gotten a new love for you.

Love: You haven't gotten it yet. The new love is not confirmed until it's sealed with a kiss.

Paul: What, a kiss? You love making my life shit.

Love: Hey, I don't make the rules; I just get amusement out of them.

Paul: I bet you do.

Love: Besides, a kiss shouldn't be that hard to get. You practically had your head in her tits.

Paul: That's a lot easier than kissing. It's odd, but it's true.

Love: Really? I'll have to keep my eye on that.

Paul: So, I have to get her to kiss me. That's just great.

Love: Yes, you have to get "her" to kiss "you." You can't kiss her. She has to kiss you.

Paul: So, she has to initiate the kiss?

Love: Bingo. Maybe you're not quite as stupid as you look.

Paul: Well, isn't this the point where you laugh at the bad news you've given me and you disappear?

Love: I was getting to it. (*Exits.*)

Paul: This is a pain in the ass.

Love:	Hahahaha (*Running on.*) I forgot to laugh at you. (*Exits.*)
Paul:	Fuck love (or Love). I'm going to have to come up with something genius for tomorrow night. Shelly is going to be pissed.

Scene III

The lights come up on Paul's room, and he's sitting on his bed. Shelly is in his room with him.

Shelly:	This is bullshit.
Paul:	That's what I said but, apparently, I have to get her to kiss me.
Shelly:	Okay, well, we have a few moves we can make, we're not beaten yet. You're having dinner with her tonight, right?
Paul:	Yeah.
Shelly:	Okay, so we get her to kiss you at dinner tonight.
Paul:	More easily said than done.
Shelly:	Look, if you want to sit here and mope, be a pansy ass and mope. Or go to dinner, win her over, get a kiss, get laid and get me back my boyfriend! In case you don't fully understand, you're not being given a choice. You are getting that kiss tonight.
Paul:	Whoa, cool down. Holy shit.
Shelly:	I can't fucking calm down. I'm not getting any, and that is a serious problem!
Paul:	All right, all right, I'll try, but I don't know how.
Shelly:	(*Grabbing the pen.*) With the pen. If you can speak like Shakespeare, you'll win her over for sure. Any girl, if she's spoken to with pure poetry, will fall for sure.
Paul:	The pen is mightier than the sword. (*Holding pen.*)
Shelly:	Well, it will be mightier than your sword.

The lights go down on Paul's room and come up on the front of the stage. There is a table set up at a restaurant with drinks and food

63

at it. Paul and Nicole are sitting at the table as the lights come up, with sounds of a restaurant.

Nicole: (*Holding her drink.*) This was a good idea.

Paul: It's easier than dancing.

          Paul pulls out the pen, looking at it.

Nicole: So, do you like reading? Do you do much reading?

Paul: Yes.

Nicole: Read anything good lately?

Paul: (*Clicks the pen three times.*) Indeed, many a time I have pondered weak and weary over many a volume of forgotten lore.

Nicole: Edgar Allen Poe.

Paul: Correct, my dear. For I love to while my time away with the bards, be it Dylan Thomas or William Blake, Alexander Pope's witty lines or Shakespeare's enchanting rhyme, or perhaps a bit of John Milton, raising the stakes.

Nicole: Wow, you've read all those people? So have I. I thought you were a science major.

Paul: True. I do dabble in the vulgarity of science, but for redemption I seek solace in the art and majesty of literature. Only their marvellous eloquence can open my soul and give me wings. (*To the audience, putting down the pen.*) Holy shit, this really works.

Nicole: So, do you like T.S. Elliot's "The Hollow Men"?

Paul: Of course. (*He picks up the pen and loses it as he accidentally flings it into the air.*)

Nicole: One of my favourites is "Second Coming" by Yates. Do you like that one?

          Paul, trying not to speak, nods and gets up, going for the pen. He grabs it and spins around.

Paul: It's a decorative way of explaining… (*Accidentally flings pen away again.*) Shit.

Nicole: Well, I guess that's one way to explain the antichrist.

Paul goes and retrieves the pen again.

Nicole: You really like that pen.

Paul: Well, what is a poet without his quill to spread his heavenly verse?

Nicole: So, you write poetry?

Paul: I do. (*Dropping the pen in a glass of water.*) Hmmmm...

Nicole: Well, that was smooth. Clearly you don't have as good motor skills as you have speech.

Paul: Well... (*Still trying to get the pen and spilling water everywhere, trying the most ridiculous method to get the pen out of the water without putting his hand in it.*) Clearly this is not working.

Nicole: So, why don't you do this? (*She sticks her hand in the glass and takes the pen.*) I'll give you the pen back after you recite me a poem you've written.

Paul: Can't I have the pen back first?

Nicole: No, recite.

Paul: Oh, no. Okay. Hickory Dickory Dock/ The bitch was sucking my cock/ The clock struck two/ I blew my goo/ And dropped her off at the next block.

Nicole: Right...well that was...

Paul: (*Grabbing the pen.*) Awful. It was absolutely awful. I can, however, give you a really fantastic one. On a lonely night I sat alone/ All quiet, alone, forlorn/ (*Accidentally flings pen at Nicole.*) Oh crap, are you all right?

Nicole: I'm all right, I suppose. Continue the poem.

Paul: But I need the pen.

Nicole: (*Handing him the pen.*) Here.

Paul:	As I sit by a dying fire/ I find my mind upon a pyre/ No freedom will I find/ Except for… (*Nicole grabs the pen.*)
Nicole:	Go on, keep the poem going.
Paul:	I…
Nicole:	Make something rhyme.
Paul:	Today I found I lost a buck/ Oh dear God, what the fuck.
Nicole:	You're tricking me somehow. You aren't a poet, are you? You can't probably even read anything in verse.
Paul:	I read "Green Eggs and Ham."
Nicole:	(*Getting up.*) No, there is something going on, I know there is.
Paul:	Wait, Nicole. (*Getting up to follow her.*)
	The lights fade on the restaurant and come up on a street lamp. Nicole and Paul are outside.
Nicole:	(*Turning on Paul.*) So, tell me what's going on, and tell me now.
Paul:	Okay, I'm not a poet, that was bullshit. But I only wanted to impress you, 'cause I know my dancing didn't.
	Shelly and Mark are seen starting to walk out on stage, and Paul notices them.
Paul:	Kiss me.
Nicole:	What?!
Paul:	Just kiss me now, please.
Nicole:	Are you out of your mind?
Paul:	No damnit, kiss me!
Nicole:	What the hell is the matter with you?!
Mark:	Paul!

Shelly: Oh, shit! (*Holding Mark.*)

Paul: Kiss me!

Nicole: What is going on?

Paul: Kiss me!

            Mark breaks loose and runs to Paul and kisses him. Paul turns his head in time and is kissed on his cheek.

Mark: Was it good for you?

Paul: Get the fuck off of me. (*Pushing him off.*)

Mark: But I love you, baby.

Paul: Shut up!

Nicole: What the fuck is going on?

Shelly: A lot. A lot of very bad things.

Paul: Look, I'll explain.

Nicole: Another rational explanation?

Paul: Look at this, do you think there is a rational explanation? No, my explanation is going to be irrational, crazy, and completely true.

Shelly: I am sure I can back the insanity up.

Mark: Paul, I have to tell you something. Ever since my eyes fell on you, in fact, even before they did, I've been in love with you.

Nicole: Wait, Mark, this is that Paul you were talking about in the coffee shop?

Mark: Yes, he's my fine hunk of man meat.

Paul: No, I'm not. I am also going to tell you why you love me. It's because of a love potion. Shelly, go get the kit.

Shelly: You got it. (*Exits.*)

Nicole: A love potion? (*Sarcastically.*)

Paul: Yes, I know it sounds like a lie, but it's true. I assure you. You see, that day, I thought the coffee was yours. I was going to put the potion in your coffee, only it ended up being his.

Nicole: He seemed to act weird out of nowhere. I thought it was drugs.

Paul: In a way. (*Shelly re-enters, holding the magic kit.*)

Shelly: Here it is.

Paul: (*Grabbing the potion bottle.*) See? Look. It was a love potion.

Nicole: So, wait. You were going to make me drink a love potion, so you could have me all over you?

Paul: Well, it didn't work. Instead I got him chasing me, trying to hammer one up my ass. So, I used some other items in the box, trying to win your heart. Like the pen, because I know you like poetry. And I tried to start learning to dance, since I knew you loved dancing.

Shelly: Yeah, Mark taught him.

Mark: I will never forget our night together.

Nicole: All these tricks and lies.

Paul: Hey, I danced with him for you.

Nicole: You also danced with a blow up doll. Was that for me too?

Paul: Well, sort of.

Nicole: Well, how did you know all those things about me?

Paul: Well, I…

Shelly: He used the invisibility dress in the magic kit.

Nicole: An invisibility dress?

Paul: (*To Shelly.*) You shouldn't have said that.

Shelly: You said you wanted to tell the truth.

68

Paul:	Well, maybe, pieces of it.
Nicole:	So, you went invisible and snuck into my room and spied on me. You went through my stuff. You invaded my privacy.
Paul:	Hey, I wore a dress for you.
Nicole:	It was invisible! So who gives a shit? I can't believe what you've done. Get away from me. (*Goes and stands over to the side.*)
Paul:	That's it, we're fucked.
Shelly:	Get over there and fix it.
Paul:	Like I can.
Mark:	Well, if she won't take you, I will. Come give me some love.
Paul:	Thank you, Mark, you gave me just the motivation I needed. Shelly, keep a leash on him. (*Paul goes over to Nicole.*)
Nicole:	Leave me alone.
Paul:	Wait, please listen to me. I've looked like an ass, I've acted like an ass, but it was all worth it just to get near you. I truly do love you. You're graceful, intelligent, fun, and you make me a better person.
Nicole:	I'm sure the writers from Dawson's Creek are ready to sue.
Paul:	Look, I'm horrible with women.
Nicole:	No shit.
Paul:	But I am not insensitive. After all, one of my favourite movies is "When Harry met Sally".
Nicole:	That's another lie. You're just saying that because you saw the movie in my room.
Paul:	"Men and women can't be friends, because the sex part always gets in the way."
Nicole:	Quote another line.
Paul:	Yes… yes... oh yes, yes, yes, yes!

Nicole:	(*To audience.*) Figures.

Paul:	Look, I've never been good with words. I'm a man of action, even if sometimes they are shitty actions. So, this is what I have to do. (*Paul grabs her and starts dancing with her.*) Nicole, I truly am in love with you. I screwed up, and I will most likely do it again.

Shelly:	Oh, you will.

Paul:	But I adore you. I'd do anything for you, and you bring out the best in me. And to prove the point, I'm dancing.

Music starts playing, and Nicole and Paul dance flawlessly. Shelly and Mark start dancing too, and Mark occasionally tries to grab a hold of Paul, but Shelly stops him. The music stops and so does their dancing.

Nicole:	Paul, I... I'm going to take a lesson from you. No more words, just action. (*She kisses Paul.*)

Paul:	You mean, you forgive me?

Nicole:	Before I answer, was what just happened another trick, or more magic?

Paul:	No, it was all me.

Nicole:	What about the music?

Love enters.

Love:	Okay, that was me.

Paul:	I did it, I did it without magic.

Love:	I noticed. Good job. (*To the audience.*) I'll chalk this one up to divine intervention.

Shelly:	So, does this mean I can get Mark back?

Love:	Yes, I'll remove the effects of the potion. I just have to draw it out of him with a kiss.

Shelly:	Holy shit, everyone gets to kiss my boyfriend but me! Why does it

have to be a kiss?

Love: Hey, I'm love.

            Love kisses Mark, and he blinks a few times and looks at Paul.

Mark: Oh God. I… You… We. Let's just not even talk about it.

Paul: I agree. I think we should never talk about it.

Mark: I didn't kiss you.

Paul: We didn't dance.

Mark: I didn't grab your ass.

Nicole: You're both talking about it.

Shelly: Yeah, stop talking I have something more important for you to do. (*Shelly grabs Mark and kisses him.*) Okay, time for us to go home.

Mark: (*As they're leaving.*) Just tell me one thing. If I was gay, I could do better than that, right? (*Pointing to Paul.*)

Shelly: Oh yeah. (*They exit.*)

Paul: (*To Love.*) Well, thanks for making my life Hell.

Love: It was a pleasure.

Paul: I'm sure it was.

Nicole: I suggest we get going. I could go with some more Tangoing.

Paul: At the club?

Nicole: No, in the bed. Let's go. (*Exits.*)

Paul: (*To audience.*) She doesn't even know I saw her topless.

Nicole: What?!

Paul: (*Running off stage.*) Nothing.

Love: Well, I guess I've done my job. (*Goes over to the magic kit on the ground and pulls out the Viagra and shakes it.*) Can't let this go to

71

waste. This shit is magic. (*Sticks Viagra in her pocket and walks offstage. The lights fade out.*)

THE SHOW

A note on *The Show*

This script marked my directorial debut. It was originally produced for the Sears Drama Festival in 2005. It was an exciting moment in my life, as the script won the Provincial Young Author's Award, and I won an Excellence Award for my directing. My favorite comment I received about the show was when one of the judges described the fight scene I choreographed as being "Tarantino" in style. Quentin Tarantino is one of my favorite Hollywood writer and directors.

One of the most interesting points I found in this show was the diversity of things I got to tackle as a director and that my cast got to tackle as performers. Every cast member had to play multiple roles as well as learn dance choreography and fight choreography. My choreographer, Katrina Laquian, was unafraid to put the cast to the test and won an Excellence award for her Choreography as well. I and my production team also changed the one male role to a female one, because we had a lack of male cast. I will not lie, this first production was hell to get put on stage but, once we did, it was worth it, and it was a very good show. I look forward to getting to run it again in the future and see what comes of it.

There were definite times when I had trouble getting my cast to listen, and before the end I had tried many different methods of getting my cast to work for me, from giving rewards of pizza at rehearsal so people would come, to holding a somber meeting where I explained that if they didn't pull their act together, I would cancel the show, or the one rehearsal when I got so angry I shattered a wooden cube with one kick. My cast was utterly silent and well-behaved for the rest of that day. I also had to replace one role about three times. I was a high school student leading other high school students. It was a challenge at best. The following is the original casting of the production:

Brent Cotter - Narrator 1
Stephanie Pellazari - Narrator 2
Nick Pigozzo - dying man, Moses, ninja, and dancer
Jake Rivers - mule, Pharaoh, ninja, and dancer
Martin Saliba - robber, slave, secret agent, and dancer
Joseph Pagnan - a man in love, slave, ninja ,and dancer
Jocelyn Rivers - a vampire, priest, ninja, and dancer
Jessica Kelly - nurse, slave 1, ninja, and dancer
Alyssa Merrick - nurse, slave 2, ninja, and dancer
Dayna Edwards - sheriff, slave, ninja, and dancer
Emily Direto - woman in love, slave, ninja, and dancer
Jennifer Pepper - woman confronted by a vampire, slave, female agent, and dancer

Characters

Narrator 1
Narrator 2
Dying Man
Moses
Mule
Pharaoh
Robber
Vampire
Priest
Sheriff
Man In Love
Woman Confronted by Vampire
Female Agent
2 Nurses
7 Slaves
Ninjas
10 Dancers

The Show

The stage is black, and two stools are preset on the side of the stage. The sound of music arriving from the distance ("Jungle Boogie") will be heard, and then it will stop. The sound of car doors opening and closing. The spotlight will go on to the stools, and Narratorw 1 and 2 will enter.

Narrator 1: I can't believe you just did that. You are fully aware that we are going to lose our jobs.

Narrator 2: Maybe not. Besides I'm getting old enough to be a has-been, but I can't even be called that. I am going to be old and unsuccessful. It's got to be one or the other, and I can't stop the getting old, so I have to get success.

Narrator 1: Oh, you're right! We can easily fulfill your promise! Don't worry, Mr. Producer, we'll have a completely original show idea by tomorrow, which everyone will want to see, and if we don't you can fire us, and give our spot to yet another reality show! (*Pulls out a flask and takes a drink.*)

Narrator 2: You're being far too dramatic. It's really not that hard. (*Takes the flask.*) Besides, I will not let us be replaced by another reality TV show, the lack of creativity in modern media ends tonight!

Narrator 1: You're right. It also explains why the people who accomplish that feat get rich and famous and win Oscars and awards! It's official: we're getting replaced by Survivor, Hawaii edition! (*Grabs the flask back.*)

Narrator 2: You know, we might have a better idea of coming up with an original idea if we actually tried to think about one.

Narrator 1: (*Puts flask away.*) Okay, where do we start?

Narrator 2: I think we should do a comedy. Everybody likes comedies.

Narrator 1: No, comedy is way overdone. Besides it's not original. We should do the opposite, tragedy. (*Tragedy music starts, "Dream On".*)

Narrator 2: Tragedy! We've never done a tragedy.

Narrator 1: How hard can it be? I can see it now. There is a bed, and a dying sick man.

Lights go up on the rest of the stage, and the sick man is lying in bed. Two nurses are not standing far off and look as though they are talking, and then their voices become audible.

Nurse 1: It's so sad, what a poor man.

Nurse 2: I know, this virus is a new one and deadly.

Nurse 1: It's a rare case to get it in the States, though.

Nurse 2: He didn't get it in the States. He got it in Africa. He was on a mission helping to build a school.

Nurse 1: We should do something that would help cheer him up. (*Pause.*) I know. We could get him a dog! I'll go to find one right now.

Both nurses exit and then Nurse 1 enters shortly after, holding a stuffed dog, and walks over to the sick man sobbing.

Nurse 1: I'm sorry, I went and got you a puppy, but on the way back he got hit by a car.

She lays the dog on the bed and walks away. The sick man has a sad look as he looks over the leash, and nurse 2 enters holding a letter. She is sobbing once again as she approaches the bed.

Nurse 2: I'm so sorry. I have a letter I think you should read. (*She walks away.*)

Sick man: (*Picks up letter and starts reading it.*) Oh no, my parents are dead. They died on the plane ride to the vacation I bought them. This is how I'm rewarded. I help kids in Africa, and that's going to kill me. I gave a gift to my parents and it killed them. (*Becoming very upset.*) Even my dog was killed!

Narrator 1: Then they discover a cure, (*Nurse 2 comes in with a needle*) but before it can be administered, the nurse has a heart attack. (*Nurse 2 complies, and at this point the only sound that is heard is Narrator 2 laughing. The lights go down, except for the spotlight on the narrators, and Narrator 2 is still laughing.*)

Narrator 2: The only way people will cry at that show is because of tears of pain of having to watch it.

Narrator 1: Well, what do you suggest oh "old" and "wise" one?

Narrator 2: Like I said before, comedy would be a real winner.

Narrator 1: No, it is not original. We need something really different, really creative. If we can't be immortal through our not dying, then it has to be through our work!

Narrator 2: Wait, I have a good idea! We can do a western! (*Western music starts playing "The Good the Bad and the Ugly Theme" and the lights go up on the rest of the stage and a couple fake cactus move onto the stage.*) We can bring back the style made famous by John Wayne and Clint Eastwood. You know, the whole, "Do you feel lucky punk?" thing.

Narrator 1: He was a cop when he said that.

Narrator 2: So? That's beside the point.

Narrator 1: Plus, it has to be original, so we can't make it like Clint or The Duke.

Narrator 2: We won't!

Narrator 1: But you just said—

Narrator 2: Shut up, I'm on a roll. First, we will have a female sheriff. (*She enters, looking brave and courageous*) But she won't be an ordinary sheriff, because instead of a horse she'll ride a mule. (*The mule enters and forces itself under the sheriff, who looks rather surprised.*) The best part is, we will do the story from the point of view of the mule. Now that's creative!

Sheriff: Let's go, mule, we have to go after those robbers. The Desert Coyotes are going to pay for messing with my town. They took all the money from the bank, and I swore on my life I would get it back. The people of Dodge City are depending on us, and we won't fail them, Yah! (*The mule sits down and the sheriff slides off his back.*) What are you doing? We have to go!

Mule: I'm not going anywhere!

Sheriff: Why?

Mule: I have a few complaints about how I'm being treated. You see, I have noticed some differences between the way the horses are treated and the way I am. They get oats and I, I get hay. They get a stable, I get an outdoor pen. They get groomed, I get ignored.

Sheriff: Now is not the time to discuss this.

Mule: Actually, now is when you actually need me, so now is the perfect time to discuss it.

Sheriff: All right, I'll compromise. I'll give you oats and the occasional grooming, but I can't build a stable.

Mule: Let me think about this

Now the Mexican robber enters, holding his gun, and stands behind the mule, who is thinking.

Robber: Don't think about going anywhere, Sheriff. I've got you right where I want you.

Sheriff: *(Reaches for a gun that isn't there and then speaks to the audience)* Now I'm starting to see the problem with being opposed to guns.

Robber: *(Starts to laugh)* Say hello to my little friend. Now you die! *(Just as he is about to shoot, the mule stops thinking and kicks him in the crotch, and he goes down.)* Right in the kookaraches.

Mule: It's a deal.

Narrator 1: This is pretty good. So what happens next? *(Narrator 2 pauses for a few moments and then shrugs his shoulders.)* So much for that idea. *(Lights go back to just the spotlight on the narrators)* That's okay, though. I came up with another idea. We can do horror! *(Horror music starts playing " Red Dragon Theme".)* This is perfect, because not a lot of people have done really good horrors on stage, and ours will be awesome.

Narrator 2: I have never heard of a horror winning an award and captivating all ages.

Narrator 1: Just work with me. I'm being original. This is what I see happening: a woman is waiting at a bus stop. It's late, and then a vampire enters.

Lights go up on the rest of the stage, a woman is standing by bus stop sign, and the vampire is slowly approaching her.

Vampire: Do you have the time? (*The woman turns her head to look at her watch and the vampire slowly leans in to try to bite her but she turns back before he can.*)

Woman: It's five after midnight. (*She looks over the strange man next to her, and then there is a rustling off to the side, and she looks in that direction and again and again the vampire leans in to try to bite her, but she turns back around in time.*) What are you doing?

Vampire: I am attracted to your...

Woman: You're being a bit too forward.

Vampire: Blood.

Woman: What? Get away, you sick freak!

Vampire: (*Grabs one of her arms and pulls her close.*) I want to feed!

Narrator 1: Then she pulls out a wooden stake. (*Woman complies with what is said.*)

Narrator 2: Wait, this has to be a family show, we can't have all kinds of blood. Besides, why would she carry one in her pocket? Maybe a little too convenient and unreal.

Narrator 1: Fine, forget the stake. (*The woman drops it.*) She pulls out a Discman. (*woman complies, and then she presses the play button, and the "Monster Mash" starts playing. The vampire starts dancing.*)

Narrator 2: And now you successfully killed the horror feel, not to mention everyone hates that song. (*Lights go back to just being the spotlight on the narrators.*) I still feel that comedy would be an excellent choice.

Narrator 1: No, I've told you a hundred times, it's been far too overdone! Besides, we could change it to the Macarena. Wveryone loves that song.

Narrator 2: No, it's not scary. Are you so thick you don't understand the concept of horror?

Narrator 1: Well, I must admit I haven't seen a whole lot. I don't like getting scared, but I'm getting scared about keeping our job due to a lack of ideas. Wait, another one just came to me. We could do an epic!

(*"Poor, Poor Pharaoh" begins.*) We could do it about Moses!

Lights go up on the rest of the stage, and Moses is standing on one side with the slave confronting the Pharaoh. There are three flats in the background, forming an Egypt scene.

Moses: Let the people of God go, or you will feel his wrath.

Pharaoh: They are the slaves of Egypt, and that is what they will stay.

Slaves: Moses, do something!

Moses: (*Lifts up the staff.*) Then God will stretch out his finger and block the sun (*Stage lights dim, and the Pharaoh looks worriedly at the Priest.*)

Pharaoh: Explain this!

Priest: Do not worry. His God has no power here. It is only coincidence.

Pharaoh: Tell your people that their God and you have just gained them double the workload. (*Pharaoh leaves.*)

Priest: Horus and Osiris, bring us back our light! (*Nothing happens. The priest looks to Moses and then to the sky, then fearfully walks away.*)

Slave 1: What a wonderful job you did to save us. We should thank you for your efforts and what it gained us. (*A couple of slaves attack Moses.*)

Slave 2: Stop! (*They listen.*) Moses tried to help, and he doesn't plan to give up, do you?

Moses: No, you will be free, and let us hope that the Pharaoh does not pay a terrible price before you are.

Narrator 2: Have you ever heard of "The Ten Commandments"? (*Lights go out, and it's back to a spotlight on the narrators.*)

Narrator 1: You made me lose my train of thought, and yes I've heard about "The Ten Commandments". It's that movie about Moses.

Narrator 2: Yah! That Oscar winning movie about Moses.

Narrator 1: Oh, I see what you're getting at. Another idea of mine fails. Fine, then I guess we're doomed. We won't do it. Maybe we haven't lost our touch. Maybe, like you said, we never had it. I need a drink! (*Pulls out flask.*)

Narrator 2: Well, what about a romance? (*Narrator 1 looks at Narrator 2 for a moment then takes another big swig.*) There can be the woman waiting for her love in the park.

Romantic music starts playing ("Can you feel the love tonight"), and the lights go up on the rest of the stage. A woman enters across the stage, and a bench has been placed behind her. Then the man enters through the house and goes up the stairs of the stage.

Man: Marry me! Marry me!

The woman turns upon hearing this and then runs into the man's arms.

Woman: I love you. You have been so good to me, and you are so special. (*To the audience*) And rich!

Man: I love you, too. You're the most beautiful woman I have ever seen. Your hair, your eyes, your smile, oh, you have something in your teeth. (*Woman reacts.*) I may be broke now, but I have you.

Woman: (*Moves away.*) You're broke?

Man: I lost everything trying to find you. I mean, since we got separated on the train, I ended up in Italy. Then I had to take a plane to France where you were supposed to be, but you weren't there. Then I had to go to—(*stopped by the woman.*)

Woman: Let me save you a long story by saying, I can't marry you.

Man: What? What do you mean?

Woman: Freeze! (*Puts up hand and man freezes, to audience.*) He's a quick one, isn't he? Show me the money! (*Man unfreezes*)

Man: But everything you just said, was it a lie?

Woman: No, but your money is why I started going out with you.

Man: Can't you get past that? Don't you have some feelings for me?

Woman: I do. I'm just nervous, but of course I do. I truly love you, and I'll
            marry you. (*She runs and goes to kiss him.*)

Man: Freeze! (*Puts up hand and woman freezes, to audience*) This is
            what Mummsie meant when she said I'd never understand a
            woman.

Narrator 1: (*Still drinking from the flask, and the alcohol is beginning to show
            its effects.*) This idea may be decent, if you only wanted women in
            the audience. We have to have something better. (*Lights go back to
            just the spotlight on the narrators.*) We have to do something that
            will keep them watching intensely, not to mention how it is dis-
            playing the woman.

Narrator 2: You mean, actually showing it truthfully, and that is how they are?

Narrator 1: You're hopeless. Maybe I should try tragedy again. I can base it
            around you; you're sad and pathetic. Besides, we don't want real-
            ity. I will not make the next reality TV show.

Narrator 2: Fine, you come up with the idea then.

Narrator 1: (*Excited and slightly drunk.*) Action!, We should do an action
            show!

            *Lights go up on the rest of the stage, and the male and female
            agents are walking across the stage.*

Agent: Well, this is Hang Chow's secret base. Now we have to find the
            plans for that new secret weapon he's building. (*At this point eight
            ninja's enter from the opposite side*) Sheila, go and find the plans,
            and I'll take care of this problem.

            *Female agent nods and exits. Then "Mission Impossible Theme"
            starts playing and the fight scene begins. They start fighting hand
            to hand and then move to using swords and at the end of the song
            the ninja's have been defeated.*

Narrator 2: So, what is so original about this?

Narrator 1: I'm getting to that.

            Female agent reenters, holding a gun and a CD.

Agent: Good, you got the plans. (*The female agent points the gun at him.*)

Female Agent: Yes, but you won't get it. You see, I work for Hang Chow!

Agent: Traitor! I'll deal with you.

Narrator 2: That's not original. Lots of times the sidekick betrays the hero.

Narrator 1: I know. This is the original part.

Agent: Did last night mean nothing to you?

Female Agent: From China with love. (*Female agent shoots the secret agent.*)

Narrator 1: How often does the hero get shot?

Narrator 2: There's a reason for that. What happens once he's dead? (*Lights go back to just the spotlight on the narrators.*) That show would have also been far less appealing to women. We need to come up with a theme that all the sexes will enjoy, something that will get them up in the aisles. Hey, everyone gets up and dances to a good song. We could use music, I think we should do a musical.

Narrator 1: A musical, that is another style that we have no experience with. Not to mention I believe that style will be tougher to try than horror or tragedy.

Narrator 2: It can't be that hard. Besides, if you don't say yes to this, we're doing comedy. Just imagine the big opening dance number.

Lights go up on all the stage and all ten actors are in position. Then a very fast paced and impressive dance number is performed to Gloria Estefen's "Conga".

Narrator 1: This is it; this is the one. We have a spectacular dance number. Now, what do we do for the storyline? (*Both the narrators pause, trying to think, but both come up blank, and the lights go back to just the spotlight on them.*)

Narrator 2: I have an idea.

Narrator 1: We are not doing comedy.

Narrator 2: No, we can use all our ideas.

Narrator 1: What do you mean?

Narrator 2: Well, we can do a show about creating a show. We can show all the ideas while we're trying to create it.

Narrator 1: That's it! It's perfect! We have to go tell the producers. It looks like the "Survivors" are staying home. We're going to be rich and famous!

Narrator 2: Maybe even win an Oscar!

"There's No Business Like Show Business" starts playing, both narrators exit, and the spotlight goes off.

PARKING LOT

PARKING LOT

A note on *Parking Lot*

A point I would like to talk about for this script is that of conception. At first when I conceived this idea, I thought I would write it as a script for film. I thought it would be intriguing to have a film in which the majority of the plot occurred in a parking lot. So many different people converge and can come together in a parking lot. I must also admit that part of me has always imagined it would be wonderful to bring the spectacle or visual feast that film can often bring to theatre. I have often heard my peers talk about why they should pay to see a play when the ticket for a movie costs the same, and so much more can be offered by film that you cannot produce on a stage. This is part of the trend of audiences, it is often lowest common denominator entertainment, and everyone seems to just want the flash and limited substance.

My main hope with this script was to take that flash and spark that film seems to have with audience and try to place it on the stage. At this point the play has never been produced on stage, but one day, sooner rather than later, I will be producing it, and then the script and concept behind it will have its real test. The arguments surrounding theatre vs. film are varied and wide, and both sides hold compelling and true points. Do I prefer one over the other? I love them both; I have done work with both, and I plan to continue to do work with both so long as I am alive. At the moment, though, I have more experience with theatre, and my funding is more suited for pursuing it than film. That is why I seem to do more work on stage rather than on camera.

Characters

Mel: A high-strung criminal who has a quick temper.

Tommy: A relaxed and calculating criminal who is easily annoyed by his partner, Mel.

Jeff: A man in love with a married woman.

Madison: A woman having an affair and who is terrified of her husband.

Eddie: A sleazy private investigator

Tracy and Rosie:
            Two undercover police officers who feel the job is the most important thing in life.

Chelsey, Sandra, Jack and Joy:
            A group of teenagers who hold the arrogance and ignorance of youth and like to get high.

Terchek and Alexis:
            Two russian drug dealers who hate America.

Captain: The police Captain

Two Robbers/Two Cops:
            As described, two actors will play both pairs.

Parking Lot

The stage is set in darkness with two men sitting in what appears to be a car down stage right. The lights go up on the car, and Tommy and Mel are sitting in it. They are listening to "Back in Black" until the car ignition gets turned off.

Narrator: 5:30 am

Mel: It's 5:30 in the morning. Tommy? Tell me you didn't get me up just to park a car here at 5:30 in the morning. You did, didn't you? *(Pause.)* So, what are we going to do? We just gonna wait here? We are, aren't we? We're just going to fucking wait here.

Tommy: Yep.

Mel: When do we do this?

Tommy: 5:00

Mel: Christ! This is stupid. This is real stupid.

Tommy: Relax, Mel.

Mel: Relax! What if word got out? We're a pretty wide open target. Two guys sitting in a car with 10.8 million dollars.

Tommy: No one knows.

Mel: Oh Yeah! What makes you so sure?

Tommy: If anyone knew, we'd already be dead. It's 10.8 million dollars, wide open, with two guys just sitting in a car.

Mel: Maybe not. Maybe they're getting sleep, Tommy! *(Pause.)* This is too public of a place to be doing this. How do you possibly think we're going to get away with this?

Tommy: No, see, that's the beauty of this plan. It's big and in the open. It's right under everyone's noses and right where no one is looking for it. At five everyone is leaving work and going home, everyone's mind is in a different place from where they are. There will be a lot of movement in the parking lot. The Russians park next to us, we give them the money, they give us the coke, and by 5:15 we're on the road with rush hour traffic, and no one knows what happened.

Mel: Won't someone get suspicious seeing a couple of cars parked here all day? What time are the Russians coming, anyway?

Tommy: Before 12:00, and no one will get suspicious. This is a big shopping plaza, I guarantee no one else will notice. Everyone who works here doesn't know everyone else's car. They'll assume it's an employee car and, if we don't sit in it all day, we really won't arouse suspicion. It'll be fine.

Mel: Yeah, so long as nothing goes wrong.

Tommy: What could go wrong? It's a big piece of asphalt.

Mel: I don't know but, Murphy's law, if it can go wrong, it will go wrong. Man, I'm hungry.

Tommy: That restaurant opens at 9:00. We can get something to eat then.

Mel: And what do we do until then?

Tommy: Sleep?

Mel: You can sleep in a car?

Tommy: If you shut up I can. (*Tommy puts his chair back and goes to sleep, and Mel tries. He tosses around for a couple minutes, and it doesn't work, so he sits back up.*)

Mel: Fucking 5:30am.

           The lights go down on Tommy and Mel and come up on the car centre stage right where Jeff is sitting. He pulls out a cigarette and lights it.

Narrator: 8:40am.

Jeff: (*Thought track through sound system.*) Where is she? She always comes to work this way. She should be here soon. Maybe she's running a late.

           Madison starts walking across the front of the stage.

Jeff: Madison! over here.

Madison looks around nervously and begins walking over to him.

Madison: Jeff, we have to talk.

Jeff: About what?

Madison: (*Looks around again.*) Let's get in the car.

Light goes down on Jeff and Madison comes up on car centre stage left. Eddie is sitting in the car, snapping pictures with a camera.

Eddie: You two make this too easy.

Lights go down on Eddie and up on car down stage left with two undercover police officers in it, Rosie and Tracy.

Rosie: Tracy, can I ask you a question?

Tracy: Well we're partners. It would be a pretty bad partnership if I said no.

Rosie: Does Mark ever bug you about the job? Do you guys ever fight about it?

Tracy: No, we don't fight about it, not out loud. It's more of a silent fight. I know he sometimes wishes I didn't have the job, but he never says anything. It's just a look he can have.

Rosie: The great thing about a look is you can look away.

Tracy: I take it Zack has been riding you about the job?

Rosie: A lot. He wants me to get out, find something safer, get a desk job. Some bullshit like that.

Tracy: You're lucky, Rosie. He loves you.

Rosie: Yeah, nothing says I love you like a yelling match as you walk out the door in the morning.

Tracy: Maybe you should?

Rosie: What?

Tracy: Get a different job. Undercover may not be the best place for you. The force has other positions.

Rosie: Do you see this badge? (*Pulls out her badge.*) It says 'to serve and protect'. How the hell do I do that from behind a desk? I love the job, I live for it.

Tracy: Well, do you love him? Because, if so contemplate that everyday you come to work, you may not see him when you go home, because you may not go home.

Rosie: Now you're sounding like him. (*Pause.*) Shit, you're just playing with my mind.

Tracy: You make it too easy.

Rosie: Give up the job. (*Laughs to herself.*) It's great to be a cop.

Tracy: Not today. Undercover and no idea who or when this deal is going down, just the place, and we get to sit here all day.

Rosie: Yeah, but think of the bust, roughly $10 million worth of coke?

Tracy: Yeah.

Rosie: The assholes won't know what hit them.

           The lights go down on the two officers and up on Jeff and Madison.

Madison: We have to call this off.

Jeff: What do you mean?

Madison: I mean it's over. I'm sure Jason suspects something.

Jeff: Let him suspect. He doesn't know anything.

Madison: It's not worth running the risk of him finding out. He'd kill us. (*Jeff brushes this off.*) I'm not kidding. You don't know Jason when he's mad. I do. I know better than to make him angry. We have to call it off.

Jeff: Look… (*Cut off by Madison.*)

Madison: No, don't start. Right now you'd say anything so that I'd keep sleeping with you.

Jeff: Will you listen to me? (*Madison relaxes.*) Look, I can accept if you want us to be over because you want it, but not because of him. Why end something you actually enjoy, stop seeing someone you care about, just to go back to that bastard that you're terrified of anyway?

Madison: Look, now isn't the time to talk about this and... (*Looks at the clock.*) Shit! I'm late for work.

            The lights come up on Eddie getting out of his car with the camera and going over to the couple in the car and knocking on their window.

Jeff: Yes? Can I help you?

Eddie: Actually, both of you can.

Madison: Well I'm late for work, so... (*Cut off by Eddie.*)

Eddie: It's for both of your best interests that you stay in that car.

Jeff: What?

Eddie: Unless, of course, you want your husband to know what the two of you have been up to.

Madison: What are you talking about?

Eddie: Boy, I figured people like you would be better with subtleties. My name is Eddie, and I'm a private investigator. I currently have been hired to investigate your little affair.

Jeff: You son of a bitch!

Eddie: Hey now. (*Pulls out a camera and snaps a picture of the two of them.*) You don't want that compromising photo and hundreds of others falling into the wrong hands, like your husband's.

Madison: What?!

Eddie: Yeah! All those pictures that your husband paid me to take. Some of them are real juicy, but I've been known to lose photos from time to time.

Madison: Lose photos?

Eddie: If the price is right.

Jeff: What price?

Eddie: $10,000

Jeff: (*Laughs.*)

Madison: (*Quickly.*) Wait, we should…(*Cut off by Jeff.*)

Jeff: Forget it, no way.

Eddie: All right, it's your life, or it was. (*Starts to walk to his car.*)

Madison: No, I'll pay. (*Eddie turns back.*)

Eddie: All right, I'm glad you sorted out your priorities. However, due to the insults I've had to take, I'm afraid the price has gone up to $20,000. Take it or leave it.

Madison: I don't have that much to give right now.

Eddie: Well then, I guess I'll have to deliver these photos to their rightful owner, because this is a limited time offer.

Jeff: The hell you will.

Eddie: That just closed the deal.

           At this point Jeff grabs Eddie and starts pulling him in through the car window. The two hit the steering wheel while fighting and cause the car to honk. The lights go down on them, and they freeze though sounds of the struggle and occasional honking continue. Lights come up on Tommy and Mel's car.

Mel: What the hell? What's going on!

Tommy: Some crazy ass people.

Mel: I just got to sleep!

           The lights go down on Mel and Tommy and up on Rosie and Tracy.

Rosie: Christ, what the hell are they doing? Should we move on this?

Tracy: No, let this go. We can't break cover. We have to hit the deal.

Rosie: All right, your call.

The lights go down on the officers and back up on Jeff's car, and the characters become unfrozen and are still fighting.

Eddie: Let go of me, asshole!

Jeff: Gladly, once you hand over the pictures.

Eddie: Sorry, you and your little bitch are just going to have to face the music.

Madison decks Eddie, and he falls to the ground. Jeff looks at her with surprise.

Madison: I hate clichés

Jeff gets out of the car and goes over to Eddie and kicks him a couple of times hard in the stomach. Then he grabs the camera and smashes it and takes the film.

Madison: Take a picture of me now asshole.

They both get into the car. The lights go down on them and up on Tommy and Mel.

Tommy: And you thought you were having a bad day, having to get up at 5:30 in the morning. Would you rather be him?

Mel: No, I'd rather be in my bed, at home, asleep. There go both cars. This is going to be a bad day, I can feel it. Let's go get something to eat.

The two get out of the car and walk across the stage and exit stage left. The light stays on the officers' car as they cross in front of it.

Rosie: Damn, that looked painful.

Tracy: I'd like to know what the hell that was about.

Rosie: I saw them trash a camera.

Tracy: A scene like that in the morning, a major drug deal going down later today; we should be in this neighborhood more often.

The lights go down on the officers and go up on the above platform of the stage set like a restaurant table. Mel and Tommy are sitting and looking out.

Narrator: 12:40 pm

Mel: Where the fuck are they? Where are they?!

Tommy: I don't know.

Mel: Well, they're really late!

Tommy: I know that!

Mel: I knew it, I knew something would go wrong, I knew it. This is bullshit. We got 10.8 million dollars in our trunk and... (*Cut off by Tommy.*)

Tommy: Mel! Shut up!

Mel: (*To an unseen waitress.*) Hey, can I get another coffee?

Tommy: No, no more coffee. You definitely don't need any more coffee. (*Pause.*) Where the hell could they be? What could be keeping them?

Mel: Vodka.

Tommy: What?

Mel: Well, they're Russians.

Tommy: Are you... Do you really... (*To the unseen waitress.*) Please get him another coffee.

Mel: Hey, could that be them? (*Pointing out as if watching cars in the parking lot.*)

Tommy: No, they're coming in a blue Eclipse.

Mel: What a shitty car.

Tommy: Well...

Mel: Whatever. Russians.

The lights go down on the restaurant and up on the car down centre left where four teens are sitting, Chelsey, Sandra, Joy and Jack.

Chelsey: Bust out the shit, man.

Sandra: Yeah, let's go.

Jack: All right, it's in my bag in the back there. *(They grab the bag and pull out their joints and start lighting up.)* Hey, check this out. *(Pulls out a switch blade.)*

Joy: Why did you get that? We know you won't use it.

Jack: I could use it.

Joy: Yeah, you could, but you never will.

Chelsey: I think she's saying you lack the balls.

Sandra: Hell, I know he lacks them.

Jack: Shut up!

Joy: Take a hit and shut up.

The lights go down on the car and back up on the restaurant where Tommy and Mel are sitting.

Tommy: Okay, now even I'm getting a little edgy.

Mel: A little? I'm getting real edgy. Carlos will kill us if we don't have the goods.

Tommy: Wait, I think... *(Seeming to watch a car.)* Yep, this is them.

Mel: About time! Let's go talk to those bastards.

Tommy: Let me do the talking.

The lights go down on the restaurant and up on the car down centre with Terchek and Alexis sitting in the car. Tommy And Mel approach it from stage left. Terchek has his window down and his arm hanging outside it.

Terchek: Are you the guys?

Tommy: You mean the guys who were expecting you an hour ago? Yeah, we're the guys.

Terchek: Sorry, time change. We forgot to change our watches.

Mel: You forgot to change your watches. Idiots!

Tommy: Mel.

Alexis: Who is this prick?

Mel: Prick?

Tommy: Mel! (*Regains his composure.*) He's my partner.

Mel: Go drink some vodka, you Russian bitch, you red loving commie.

Alexis: Fuck you!

Terchek: Enough!

Tommy: You're going to have to park next to us.

Terchek: Why?

Tommy: So we're not carrying the stuff across the parking lot where everyone can see, dumbass.

Terchek: You're right, that's a good idea. Which is yours?

Tommy: The brown piece of shit at the end there.

Terchek: The one that another car just pulled up next to.

Tommy: Shit. Yeah. We'll have to wait.

Terchek: We have till five.

Tommy: Keep your eyes open. When the space is free, take it.

Terchek: Yah, yah. (*Tommy nods his head and drags Mel away, and they walk back to their car. The lights go down on the Russians and follow them.*)

100

Mel:	Stupid Russians. (*Mockingly with their accent.*) Didn't set our watches.
	The lights go down on Tommy and Mel as they get in the car and come back up on Terchek and Alexis's car.
Alexis:	I hate Americans. (*Terchek nods.*)
Terchek:	Too bad they have all of the money.
	The lights go down on the Russians and up on the two officers.
Tracy:	Looks like the excitement happens early around here, because other than that fight this morning, dick all has happened.
Rosie:	Maybe we got here too late. Maybe they already did the deal.
Tracy:	I hope not. This is too good of a bust to miss.
Rosie:	Well, I guess we just keep waiting.
Tracy:	Until tomorrow?
	A couple of guys go walking by the car, and Rosie watches them through the windshield. She sees one of them putting a gun in their pants, and they walk towards a corner store in the plaza.
Rosie:	Tracy, I think we have a problem.
Tracy:	What?
Rosie:	Those guys that just walked by us, I think they're going to rob that convenience store.
Tracy:	What?
Rosie:	Those guys that just walked by us, I think they're going to rob that convenience store.
Tracy:	You're just looking too hard for action.
Rosie:	They're armed.
Tracy:	Are you sure? Because... (*A gunshot is heard from offstage.*) Oh shit! (*Rosie goes to get out of the car.*) Wait! We can't break cover.

101

Rosie:	People could be killed.
Tracy:	All right, come on! (*They get out and pull their guns and run off-stage. The stage goes black.*)
Rosie:	Freeze!
Tracy:	On the ground!
Robber:	I'll kill the clerk.

Several shots are heard. After a few moments of silence, the lights come up on Tracy and Rosie outside their car, and Rosie's arm is wrapped where she has apparently been shot.

Narrator:	2:30pm
Tracy:	God damn, what a day.
Rosie:	So much for the bust.
Tracy:	Yeah, we got a shoot out and saved a life instead. All around, I don't think I had enough fulfillment for one shift.
Rosie:	Yeah, someday. (*Putting her hand on her wound.*)
Tracy:	You should have gone to the hospital.
Rosie:	It's not that bad. Besides, I have to stick around. Have to give my witness statement.
Tracy:	Shit, they'll take that from you later. Besides, there are a lot of other statements to collect. All these cars and all these people in the lot.
Rosie:	Truth is, I wanted to think.
Tracy:	About what?
Rosie:	What Zack has been bugging me about. Maybe he's right. Maybe another job is what I should be doing. When I jumped across that doorway and I got hit, I thought I was dead. I didn't want to die. I saw Zack, and I thought, he is what matters most. Us being together is what's most important. They say you don't appreciate

what you've goy until it's gone. Well, today I got to feel what it would be like if it was gone, and I didn't like it. I'm lucky, I didn't lose it, and I don't want to.

The lights go down on the officers and up on Tommy and Mel.

Mel: We are so fucked! They're going to catch us for sure!

Tommy: They won't.

Mel: Bullshit!

Tommy: All they want are witness statements. They aren't searching the cars. So long as we don't do anything stupid, we'll be fine.

Mel: Fine! You call this fine? Look at all the cops. Even if we don't get caught, which we probably will, we still can't do the deal.

Tommy: Sure we will. The cops will clear out eventually, and we'll do it. We just have to wait them out, and that won't take too long. They'll collect the statements, clean up, clear out, and then we do the deal.

Mel: If that's the plan, shouldn't we be telling the Russians?

Tommy: No. If we go over and talk with them, then the cops may get suspicious of us, and then we are in shit.

Mel: We're already in shit. What if the Russians drive away?

Tommy: Then we're fucked.

The lights go down on Tommy and Mel and up on the kids.

Chelsey: Shit, look at all the cops.

Sandra: When they come to question us they'll smell the weed for sure.

Jack: They won't give a shit about us. They're only gonna ask us what we saw.

Joy: I know what I saw, a whole shit load of coke in that blue Eclipse's trunk.

Jack: What?!

Joy: Yeah, I saw the guy get out of the car and move it after the shooting, to try to hide it more.

Sandra: An Eclipse, what a crappy car. You'd figure a drug dealer could do better.

Joy: We should take it.

Chelsey: What?!

Joy: Yeah, it wouldn't be too hard.

Sandra: And all the cops?

Joy: We do it quick and quiet. There's four of us and two of them in the car. You have your new knife, Jack. You said you could use it. Well, here's your chance to prove yourself.

Jack: How?!

Joy: We'll go up to the car and distract them, acting like a sluts. When they're not looking, then you sneak up on the other side of the car, kill the one guy, then reach over and do the other.

Jack: It could work.

Joy: If you're man enough to do it.

Sandra: That would be a lot of money.

Chelsey: But the cops.

Joy: They're preoccupied, as is everyone else in this parking lot. No one will see.

Sandra: So, what do we do?

Joy: We go distract the guy and make the woman jealous and, while they're focused on us, Jack takes them out.

Jack: Let's do it. This is too much to pass up.

The lights go down on the kids and up on the Russians' car.

Terchek: I hate Americans, always shooting shit.

Alexis: You shouldn't have gotten out and moved the stuff.

Terchek: Had to. The cops are going to question us and, in case they poke around, I don't want them to find anything.

Alexis: What do we do about the cops?

Terchek: We wait and see what happens. If worse comes to worse, we shoot them and drive away.

Alexis: And what do we do about the deal?

Terchek: We wait until the other two tell us what's going on. (*At this point Joy walks over to Terchek's car and leans in his window with Chelsey and Sandra right behind her.*)

Joy: Hey there. You hot? Cause we are. (*She takes off her outer top and has a much more revealing one underneath. She is clearly not wearing a bra. Meanwhile, Jack makes his way along Alexis' side of the car with his switchblade out.*) You want to see a little more? (*Joy begins to remove her second shirt while Jack goes to strike Alexis. Terchek sees this and quickly pulls his gun, shoots Jack, then grabs Joy by the hair and puts the gun to her head.*)

Terchek: Stupid kids!

Chelsey and Sandra : (*Scream.*)

The lights go up on the officers as they see the scene.

Tracy: Rosie! (*She starts moving to the scene, gun drawn, and Rosie starts to follow.*)

Rosie: Put the gun down! (*Both Rosie and Tracy have their guns on Terchek. Alexis sees the opportunity and shoots twice through the windshield into Rosie. Tracy shoots Terchek a few times, and the other two cops coming up on the scene fire into Alexis. Joy is quivering by the car. The other two cops round up the kids and leave the light, and Tracy runs down to Rosie's side, where she lies on the ground*)

Tracy: Rosie, hold on, shit, hold on!

Rosie dies in Tracy's arms, and she begins to cry and shake. She looks up with intense anger and pain.

105

| Tracy: | (*Stands up and goes toward Russians' car.*) Fuck! Mother Fucker! You son of a bitch! You fucking... (*She collapses to the ground in tears.*) |

The lights go down on everything and up on Tommy and Mel's car.

| Mel: | (*While pounding the dashboard*) Stupid Russians! |

| Tommy: | Fuck me. |

| Mel: | Yeah, now we're screwed. They'll find the coke, and then they'll find us. Man! And you had to wake me up at 5:30 for this shit! |

The lights go down and come up on the Police Captain and Tracy outside her car.

| Narrator: | 6:00pm |

| Captain: | You going to be all right? |

| Tracy: | Yeah, I'll be okay. |

| Captain: | All right. I guess I better go see her husband. |

| Tracy: | No, let me do it. He has to be told right. He has to know what she said before she went. Only I can do that. Only I can make him understand. |

| Captain: | (*Trying to keep things light.*) Never send a man to do a woman's job. (*Looking concerned.*) Take all the time you need. |

| Tracy: | I won't be back. I'm transferring out. |

The captain looks and nods and then walks away. Tracy pulls out Rosie's badge, looks at it and then starts the ignition. The light goes down on the car, and it is heard driving away. The light comes up on Tommy and Mel's car.

| Mel: | I can't believe we didn't get caught. This was nuts. |

| Tommy: | I can't believe today. This morning this place was just a big piece of asphalt, but now... people have died. It became a crime scene. Like you said, it's crazy. |

Mel: That it? Are you done with your deep thought for the day? All I can say is, I'm glad we didn't have to pay to sit here all day. I need a drink.

Tommy looks at him and starts the ignition as "Running with the Devil" starts playing and the lights go out.

LOSERS AND LAWSUITS

A note on *Losers and Lawsuits*

I would like to talk briefly about conception, as I find it an amusing story that goes along with this particular piece. I came up with this story idea in a restaurant in Guelph where I was eating with a friend. I remember the two of us were sitting at the table, and he had bought three scratch tickets, which said one in three chances of winning. He scratched all three, and typical to the laws of gambling, he lost and declared the simple statement of "I should sue." From that comment, this script was born. It is interesting to get to write a comedy script that deals with the law, because I find it is an area of the world filled with humor. There have been so many ridiculous lawsuits. The law always seems to be able to take any situation, no matter how simple it is to begin with, and complicate it to a point where no one can follow.

I think the law is also one of the greatest examples that common sense has died, and we have been brought into a society where we need instructions on our pop tarts and toaster strudel boxes and a pop tart setting on our toasters. The worst result of the growing epidemic of lawsuits, however, is the number of small claims court television shows which exist—Judge Judy, Judge Alex, Jude Joe Brown, The People's Court and Judge Mathis. The only redeeming point to be found in these is that you can sit back, watch the cases, and rest assured that you are smarter than those people. Overall, this script was created just for fun, and to give people a good laugh at some of the happenings of the legal system and the strange way that the world can be viewed by the eyes of legal professionals. It is fitting that we laugh at the legal system because, in the long run, it is all we can do to keep from crying.

Characters

Clarence Devry:
> A man who is a born loser but is homely and happy and easy to like.

Melvin Arnot:
> A slick lawyer who has a sharp tongue and likes to win.

Alexis Monty:
> Another lawyer with an equally sharp tongue and who also likes to win.

Dealer: A female dealer at the casino who has feelings for Clarence.

Suit: Head of the casino.

Reporter
Vendor
Bar Tender
Person on the Street

Losers and Lawsuits

Act I

Scene I

The stage is set to be a coffee shop. There is bar seating and a man in a suit drinking a coffee and reading the newspaper. This man is Melvin Arnot. He is a lawyer and, as he is enjoying his morning, a reporter, approaches him.

Reporter: Excuse me, Mr. Arnot. I was wondering if I could talk to you for a minute.

Melvin: Are you a reporter?

Reporter: Yes, Sir.

Melvin: Well, come on over then.

Reporter: I was wondering if I could talk to you about one of your cases.

Melvin: Absolutely, I won't even put a time limit on it if you throw in a nice picture. I just love seeing my big smiling face.

Reporter: I'd recommend a mirror.

Melvin: Well, I guess I prefer everyone else seeing my big smiling face.

Reporter: You are pretty full of yourself, aren't you?

Melvin: Well, if you were as good as me, you would be too. So what did you want to talk about?

Reporter: Your case where you represented Clarence Devry.

Melvin: Ah, that one made a lot headlines in its time. Come to think of it, I have made a lot of headlines overall.

Reporter: Yes, you have. Can you tell me about the case?

Melvin: All right. Before you can understand the case and, more importantly, why I decided to take it, you have to understand Clarence.

Scene II

The lights come up on a Las Vegas casino where a number of people are playing games and milling about. There are the sounds of slot machines and people around the craps table. A man, Clarence Devry, enters from stage right and makes his way across it, sipping the drink he has in his hands. He has a terrible and loud Hawaiian shirt on and equally loud shorts. He is wearing a straw hat and socks with sandals on. He moves to an empty black jack table on stage left where there is a dealer sitting. Once he arrives, the lights go down on all the background of the casino and stay on Clarence and the Dealer. He puts his drink down and hands some cash to the dealer.

Dealer: Changing five hundred. Back again, Clarence?

Clarence: Well, my wallet was feeling a little heavy, so I thought I would lighten the load. (*The dealer deals a hand.*)

Dealer: What happens if you win?

Clarence: Hit me. I never win.

Dealer: (*Collects the chips from Clarence as he lost the last hand.*) If you never win, why do you play? (*Deals another hand.*)

Clarence: Well, there is a first time for everything, I suppose. Hit me.

Dealer: (*Collects Clarence's money again.*) What would you do if you did win?

Clarence: I think the first thing that may happen to me is heart attack. Or possibly I would get excited and then wake up in my bed to discover it was only a dream. To be quite frank, I can't even imagine winning, so what I would do if I won is a question I have never really considered. I'll stay.

Dealer: Imagine you did win, and you won big, what would you do with the money? What would you buy, where would you go? (*Collects Clarence's money again.*) I realize I am not making it easy. This is odd for a dealer, but I feel like I should be apologizing to you.

Clarence: Not at all. I am used to this. If I won...what a thought. Well, I would love to buy a nice house. (*As Clarence talks about the things he would like silhouettes of them begin to appear in black light in the centre stager and stage right.*) Yeah, that would sure beat the roach infested apartment I have now. I would get a car—oh why stop at one? I could get two or three. Well, I don't want to be greedy, so maybe just one. I could buy a chef, a good one and have five star meals cooked for me everyday. I could travel the world. I could do a lot. Of course, the thing I would like is love and a family, but money doesn't buy that. (*All of his ideas fade off of the stage.*) It's a wonderful thought.

Dealer: I am sorry to say this, Clarence, but you are out of chips.

Clarence: (*Looking down at the table.*) So I am. Well, I suppose my wallet is lighter now. I also guess tonight is not the night for me to win.

Dealer: Better luck next time to you, I hope.

Clarence: It's got nothing to do with luck. I am just a born loser. I mean, honestly, look at me. (*The Dealer does and nods her head in agreement, and then the lights come back up with the rest of the casino sights and sounds.*)

Voice over casino sound system: Welcome to Golden Corral in Las Vegas! Where everybody's a winner!

Clarence: (*Sipping his drink as he leaves.*) My foot!

Scene III

The stage is now set to be a law office. There is a poster framed above the desk in which Melvin Arnot, appears in a blown up newspaper column where the headline reads: "Arnot wins case again, lucky B$%#^!D". The office is furnished with a desk and a couple of chairs. There are some shelves and cabinets and a phone on the desk. At this point, Arnot walks into the office from a door in the flat stage left. He is holding a cardboard box, some files, a take out bag in his mouth, and a take out cup of coffee in his other hand. He tries to balance his way to his desk and almost makes it after a couple of near spills. He puts it down, the phone rings, and he grabs for it, knocking everything off his desk. He looks in disgust for a moment and then answers the still ringing phone.

Melvin: Hello. Yes, Janice I am in the office, but you know that because I just walked by you when I was coming in. Yes, that's right, it was me just a few moments ago. Well, good morning again then. (*Hangs up the phone.*) I had to hire the blonde one. (*Melvin starts to pick up all the items he had which have fallen unto the floor. He gets a number of things picked up, and the phone rings again. He goes to pick it up and knocks all of his items back onto the floor.*) Hello. Yes, Janice. No, Janice I don't need a coffee, I walked in with one. Was that everything? Really, well send him in. (*Hangs up the phone and sits behind the desk. Shortly after, Clarence walks in.*)

Clarence: This a mighty fine office you have here. Looks like the office of a winner.

Melvin: Generally I am. So, what can I do for you?

Clarence: I have a case I would like you to take.

Melvin: Well, before we go any further, can I win the case? Because that is what everything really hinges on.

Clarence: To be honest, I am not really sure. I don't have much experience with winning.

Melvin: Well, explain your case to me, and we'll see. What is it, personal injury? (*Putting his feet up on the desk.*)

Clarence: False advertising, I would say.

Melvin: Now that is intriguing. Who was been wrongfully advertising, and do they have deep pockets and a large wallet?

Clarence: Is a casino large enough? (*Melvin almost falls out of his chair.*)

Melvin: You want to sue a casino?

Clarence: Yes, I do. The Golden Corral, precisely.

Melvin: I see. If I might ask, why is it you want to sue them?

Clarence: I didn't win.

Melvin: (*Starts laughing.*) Well, I certainly hope you or joking, or I am very worried that you are wasting my time.

Clarence: No, I am serious.

116

Melvin:	I see. Well, I have to be honest with you, buddy. I only take winning cases, and this is not a case that is going to win.
Clarence:	Well, it might. Some other odd cases have won before. There is the woman that spilt hot coffee on her lap and sued the coffee shop for not saying it was hot. There was the robber who locked himself in someone's garage for about a week and sued and won, or the woman who sued the Winnebago company for saying the vehicle had cruise control but didn't instruct her that she could not go into the back and make a sandwich while it was on that particular setting.
Melvin:	All right, fair enough, you have given some decent examples. So why do you think you can sue the Casino for losing? The whole theory behind gambling is the risk, and it is a well known fact that the casino is at less risk than the player.
Clarence:	Oh, believe me, I know that.
Melvin:	So then, how do you expect to be able to sue?
Clarence:	Well, my main issue lies with the fact that the casino says that everyone is a winner.
Melvin:	How's that?
Clarence:	Yes, sir. The message they constantly play through the sound system of the casino was "Welcome to the Golden Corral Casino in Las Vegas. Where everybody is a winner." All I know is, I have never been a winner.
Melvin:	Never.
Clarence:	Not once, ever. I have never won a thing at that casino, or at any of them for that matter.
Melvin:	I see.
Clarence:	I figured, since they said I was a winner, and I never was, there would be some sort of legal grounds for a lawsuit there.
Melvin:	There may be. I am thinking I may reconsider my hasty statement about saying your case could not be won. It is of course, a stretch, but it is not an impossible one, and if any lawyer could do it, it's me.

117

Clarence: So, you'll take my case?

Melvin: Well, Sir, if your discontent at the situation wasn't enough to convince me, the money I can make off of suing the casino certainly is.

Clarence: Well, thank you sir. (*Shaking Melvin's hand.*)

Melvin: We may even make legal history together, if we win.

Clarence: That is a big if. As I have explained, winning is not my forte.

Melvin: That's just fine, because it is mine.

Scene IV

The stage is bare except for a newsstand down stage left with a Vendor and a random person on the street. The customer walks up and starts flipping through some of the papers, and the Vendor begins talking to him.

Vendor: Have you heard the news?

Person: If I had heard the news, I wouldn't be trying to read it.

Vendor: Good point. Would you like a hot dog?

Person: What?

Vendor: Well, I figured I would diversify to help make some more cash, so I am a newsstand and a hot dog stand in one. Would you like one?

Person: No. What was this news you were talking about?

Vendor: Some guy is suing a casino for losing. Can you believe it? What will people try next? Anyway, he is suing the casino because of the messages they always play. They are always saying things like, "Welcome to Las Vegas, where everyone is winner." Well, he is suing them for it, because he is always losing.

Person: Well, that's just crap. Of course he lost. Everyone knows to ignore those messages.

Vendor: So, then why do they play them?

Person: (*Pauses.*) Let me try one of those hot dogs. (*The vendor hands him one, and he takes a bite.*) This tastes like paper.

Vendor: Well, I am looking for a way to diversify my products as well.

Scene V

The stage is set to be the office of the casino head. He sits behind a desk, and a woman sits in front of him. The office has a large stylish desk devoid of knick knacks. The office is very clean, and the man who runs it has good taste and is clearly wealthy. The woman sitting in front of him is wearing a dressy skirt and blouse with a jacket. She has glasses and looks beautiful but cold. Her name is Alexis Monty, and she is a lawyer.

Suit: Alexis, you are among top in your profession, you really are. Not many lawyers have won as many cases as you. Not many lawyers are as expensive as you.

Alexis: I know, what can I say? I know what I am worth.

Suit: Well, I certainly hope so, because that case you are going to be defending me on in court is extremely important.

Alexis: Explain it.

Suit: Well, it seems some moron has decided they want to try to sue me for the friendly little message I have been sending out through the casino.

Alexis: The "everybody is a winner" thing?

Suit: Yes.

Alexis: It is such a blatant lie. Why do you play it?

Suit: Because it sounds better than "I hope you leave here broke so I can buy a new Ferrari."

Alexis: A good point.

Suit: Anyway, apparently this schmuck has never won in this casino, ever, or in any casino for that matter. And that worries me, because I do not want to be the next fool everyone talks about who lost a lot of money on something very stupid.

Alexis: That would actually be the least of your worries. If he wins the case, that sets the precedent for everyone else. Imagine how many other big time losers will come pouring through the doors of this and every casino with this lawsuit. It will get to a point where you have to say "kiss the kids' college fund goodbye" on all of your poker chips, and the craps table will have to read, "Two house mortgages aren't that bad." Just wait. If they have to write "caution hot" on a cup of coffee or "do not ingest" on a lava lamp, just wait till you see what gets done to you.

Suit: You have to win this.

Alexis: No worries there. I am not a loser. Who has he retained as counsel?

Suit: Melvin Arnot.

Alexis: I'll have to pay him a visit.

Scene VI

The stage is bare, except for a street lamp and trash can, where Melvin is standing in his coat. Alexis walks up beside him. He is messily eating a sandwich, and she watches in disgust as he tries to finish it quickly and gratefully but fails horribly and more of it ends up on him than in him.

Alexis: My name is Alexis Monty. I am representing Golden Corral in the lawsuit.

Melvin: Oh, Melvin Arnot. I am suing your client. Actually, my client is suing your client.

Alexis: I know.

Melvin: Might I also say that you have a lovely pair of legs.

Alexis: And you have a charming lack of wit.

Melvin: Unfortunately, past the legs there isn't much to write home about.

Alexis: Nice work with all the mayo. (*Pointing to it all over his jacket.*)

120

Melvin:	Probably looks like you on a Friday night.
Alexis:	Well, thank you for confirming how much of a jackass you are.
Melvin:	I thought that went without saying; I'm a lawyer. So are you, which explains why you are a cold, hard bitch.
Alexis:	You know you are going to lose this case.
Melvin:	I don't lose cases, honey. I never have, and I never will.
Alexis:	Don't call me honey.
Melvin:	Oh, did you prefer bitch?
Alexis:	Listen, jackass. I am trying to give you fair warning before we go into court and I make a fool out of you.
Melvin:	Okay, I'm listening. How are you going to make a fool out of me?
Alexis:	This whole case is based on having fun with words and terms used. It doesn't have to deal with contexts or with the realities of the world we are situated, just the words that were used.
Melvin:	More or less.
Alexis:	So, there is your fatal error. The statement was "Where everybody is a winner." That doesn't mean just inside the casino. So long as your client has won something, somewhere, this case is already closed. Then he is in fact a winner, and his case will no longer be valid.
Melvin:	I see. I didn't think of that.
Alexis:	I know. I am going to comb through your clients past and, when I find what I am looking for, this case won't even make it to court.
Melvin:	Fair enough.
Alexis:	You don't seem too worried.
Melvin:	I'm not.
Alexis:	You should be.
Melvin:	(*Laughing.*) I'm sorry, you just sounded a lot like a cartoon villain

121

right there. "You should be." You're funny. I am going to enjoy beating you. You need your balls to shrink a little.

Alexis: Well then, they will match yours.

Melvin: Well, it's been a lovely chat. Let me know what you find. (*He exits out of the light.*)

Alexis: Oh, I will. (*Lights go down.*)

Act II

Scene I

The stage is now set as a bar, and Melvin is sitting at the bar and drinking happily. It is not long before Alexis comes in, looking rather disheveled and like she hasn't slept in several days. She reaches the bar, orders a drink from the bartender and sits down next to Melvin.

Melvin: It's been a couple days. What have you found?

Alexis: You bastard. You knew, didn't you?

Melvin: No, I didn't, but I had a good guess. Come on, humor me, what did you find?

Alexis: Nothing. Not a scratch ticket or a little league game. Not a science competition or even a raffle. He has not won a single thing, ever. He hasn't even won an attendance award for anything. He has never even won a game of tag or gotten the prize in a box of cereal!

Melvin: (*Laughing to himself.*) I knew it.

Alexis: I hate you.

Melvin: I must say, I have never been so happy that I have such a pathetic client. The man is the biggest loser I have ever met.

Alexis: Well then, he has the right lawyer.

Melvin: You're right. He needs a winner like me to show him the way.

Alexis: Actually, I was thinking he picked the right lawyer because if he is such a loser, maybe he'll place some of that luck on you, jackass. What made you think that your client was such a loser?

Melvin: He wears a Hawaiian shirt, socks and sandals.

Alexis: Clearly he is straight too.

Melvin: Well, you drink up, because you are going to need it. By the way, you look terrible. (*He leaves.*)

Alexis: I am sure after a couple of drinks most of the guys here won't mind.

Bartender: (*Leaning in close.*) I won't. (*Alexis stares at him.*)

Scene II

The stage is once again set to be Melvin's office. He is behind his desk. He is on the phone as Clarence enters in to the office, walking rather slowly, and he goes and sits down in one of the chairs.

Melvin: Yes, well, thank you for informing me. Oh, I am sure you did. No, that's just fine. Oh, I will be sure to. Go to Hell! (*Hangs up the phone. For a few minutes he sits strumming his fingers on the desk, and Clarence is fidgeting.*)

Clarence: So, I guess they called you?

Melvin: They did indeed. Is it true?

Clarence: Well, let me tell you about last night. I went to Golden Corral...(*"Viva Las Vegas" starts playing, and the scene changes from the law office to the casino floor of Golden Corral again. There are a number of people back at the craps table, and Clarence makes his way to the Black Jack table, where the dealer is standing.*)

Dealer: Back yet again, Clarence. Even though you are suing the place?

Clarence: Well, I figured a little extra losing wouldn't hurt.

Dealer: I don't care what you say. I don't think you are that big of a loser. No, actually I have had my eye on you for sometime. Even with your bad luck, you always have a smile on your face, Clarence. I smile every time I see you, and I always cover this table at night for a certain reason.

Clarence: Well, any dealer would like having me at their table. They always win.

Dealer: You're right. I do always win, but not in the way you think. (*Clarence changes in his cash for some chips, and the Dealer deals a hand.*)

Clarence: What's your name?

Dealer: Monica.

Clarence: I like that name. Hit me.

Dealer: Do you remember when you said that you wished to have love and a family? Maybe I could help with that. (*Takes Clarence's chips.*) Did you want to go to one of the wedding chapels after you lose your money? (*Dealer deals another hand.*)

Clarence: I'll stay. I was thinking maybe grabbing a coffee.

Dealer: Oh, I'm sorry. I didn't mean to be pushy. I am such an idiot.

Clarence: (*Taking her hand.*) No, I didn't mean that. You just took me by surprise. I am not used to having any luck, or to winning anything, and you are a better jackpot than I could ever hope to win.

Dealer: Oh my, you are so sweet.

Clarence: You should take my chips. I lost.

Dealer: Oh. (*Rakes in his chips.*)

Clarence: This should be my last hand looking at my chips. I'll lose one more time.

Dealer: Then you will win big. (*The Dealer hands out the cards and moves in to kiss Clarence, who meets her lips and then starts flapping his arms in excitement as he looks at his cards.*)

Clarence: Black Jack! I won! I won!

Dealer: Oh my God! You did!

Clarence: I can't believe it.

Dealer: Are we still leaving?

Clarence: Yes, let's, before my luck runs out and you change your mind.

Dealer: It could never happen. (*She clings around him and kisses him one more time.*) Maybe you should try the slot machine just before we go.

Clarence: All right. (*He walks up to the slot machine and puts in a quarter. All of a sudden, the lights start flashing and then Clarence reacts with great delight.*) I won the jackpot, five million dollars!

Dealer: Oh my God. (*Grabbing hold of him and kissing him again. All the other people in the casino start crowding in around him, and the message comes over the casino sound system again.*)

Message: Welcome to the Las Vegas Golden Corral Casino, where everyone is a winner!

Clarence: It's true!!!! (*Viva Las Vegas starts playing again, and then the lights fade and the stage becomes set as Melvin's office, where he is sitting behind the desk and Clarence is sitting in the chair.*)

Melvin: Really?

Clarence: Yep. (*Shows the wedding ring on his finger.*)

Melvin: Wow.

Clarence: So, I am feeling that the only responsible option now is to drop the lawsuit.

Melvin: Yes, I would have to agree with you on that point. It would seem the only responsible thing to do.

Clarence: I do want to thank you for your time and being willing to take the case. We certainly did create a stir.

Melvin: Yes, we did.

Clarence: Well, I hope you have a good day, and maybe I'll be seeing you. (*He leaves.*)

Melvin: Well, I suppose I didn't lose.

Scene III

The stage is set with a street lamp and a trash can, and Melvin is reading the newspaper. While he is standing there, Alexis walks up to where he is standing.

Alexis: Well, Melvin. Looks like you didn't win the case.

Melvin: I didn't lose it either.

Alexis: You would have.

Melvin: You must be happy he won.

Alexis: I certainly was.

Melvin: Your client must have been happy too.

Alexis: I don't like the inference jackass.

Melvin: Sorry, I meant no offence, bitch.

Alexis: You know…(*Stops, looking at Melvin.*) Want to get a coffee?

Melvin: I was thinking a wedding chapel. Clarence did it.

Alexis: Yes, because his luck goes so well.

Melvin: Coffee sounds good.

Alexis: Then maybe you can make another mayonnaise mess. (*She exits offstage.*)

Melvin: Mayonnaise mess? Oh… I'm coming! (*Runs offstage, and the lights go down.*)

Scene IV

The stage is set again as the coffee shop from the beginning of the play. The reporter is there, talking with Melvin still.

Melvin: And that's the story of the strangest case I ever started and never really finished.

Reporter: Do you ever see Clarence?

Melvin: No, but if I see him, I have a feeling it will be to handle his divorce. Married in one night.

Reporter: So do you believe he had a case, really?

Melvin: Before he won, certainly.

Reporter: You don't think that falls in the realm of common sense?

Melvin: Maybe, but that died years ago! (*Alexis enters into the coffee shop.*)

Alexis: Melvin, are you ready?

Melvin: Yeah.

Reporter: You two are still seeing each other?

Alexis: We are. In fact, we're going into business together.

Reporter: Really. Any good cases?

Melvin: There is one that is looking promising. There is a woman suing a company for failing to explain that there is no "any" key in the computer, and they claimed their system for it was idiot proof.

Reporter: So, she is calling herself an idiot?

Alexis: Well, I'll say this, at least she is being honest.

Reporter: Who is she?

Melvin: Janice, my secretary. (*The lights fade, and "Hound Dog" starts playing.*)

MY SON

A note on *My Son*

This script I created as a way of exploring one particular character. The hope is that the actor who gets the role of Jack Tagan will really be able to take it and run. I want to see them live the role. This character is fun because, when done right, it will be the perfect mix of good and bad, and the audience will love it. He will be human, a quality that all good characters have. This script has the potential to become a wonderful character sketch and to examine the nature of people and how people are always capable of surprising you and changing. However, the other point I would like to discuss with this script is how a production must not only consider what is on the page of a script but beyond it.

I am talking about facial expressions, body language, the way a line is delivered, and the pauses the actor puts in. Often scripts will have some notes on these points, but the majority of the time a great deal must rest in the hands of the director and actors to consider. Often this is what can take a good production and make it great. This is one of those scripts where the actor intuition can lift it over the top. It all centres around Jack Tagan and that character's thoughts, emotions, reactions and opinions. The character needs other good actors to play off of, but that character is always the focus. When reading this script, every actor should look for all the ways to maximize the character and really show the audience through words and through all of their body how the characters are feeling.

I believe that there are elements of Jack that can be found in many people. I am very self critical, and I believe that has influenced the way Jack perceives to think little of himself. I also think people in general will talk about being content with where they are in life, and it is an outright lie, out of the fear of not wanting to break the zone that's become comfortable for something they more deeply desire. Every person is also able to be good or bad in a moment, and we all fight within ourselves at times as to what we consider is right, not just for us, but for others. Finally, it is safe to say every human being is looking out for another one, even if it is in a misguided way. So, when the script is read, see what elements you may see from yourself or someone you know in Jack and his defense mechanisms and feelings.

Characters

Josh Brand:
> A talented young criminal who becomes a cop.

Jack Tagan:
> An older and experienced criminal who seems content but longs to be more and to prove, even if only to himself, he is not a lost soul.

Vincent: A crime boss and murderer.

Detective: A police detective with attitude.

Two Thugs

My Son

Scene I

The stage opens with sounds of passing traffic and inner city sounds. The stage is set to resemble a back road or alley way. There are flats with several back entrances to restaurants and various shops. Some various crates and a trash can are sitting along the alley wall, and there are various pieces of litter or bundles of newspapers. Two men enter onto the stage, Jack Tagan and Josh Brand. Jack is in his mid-forties, and Josh is in his early twenties. Both men are dressed in jeans, and each wears a jacket. Their body language is calm but cautious, and they are checking over their shoulders as they move on stage. Josh has his hands in his pockets, and Jack is wearing sunglasses.

Jack: Not bad kid, not bad at all.

Josh: You think?

Jack: Yeah, you have talent.

Josh: Well, I know that. (*He stops, and so does Jack, and they lean against the wall. Jack lights a cigarette.*)

Jack: I have to admit, I am impressed at how collected you were on the job. Your plan worked exactly as you thought it would. I have never seen as quick a lift as you made on that manager. He passes you and, just as he walks by, you slip his keys off his belt. One quick smooth motion. Then, once you have the key, you slip in the back while I keep everyone in place, pull the gun and rob the register and a couple smaller pieces out front. Meanwhile, you sneak out the back with the real big stuff. I run out the front, and then we meet up a couple blocks away. It's beautiful. No blood, no mess, easy clean. You must love the thrill.

Josh: Hell yeah!

Jack: So, let me see those stones.

Josh: Here they are. (*He pulls out a black cloth filled with diamonds.*)

Jack: Okay, hand them here kid. (*Josh hands him the diamonds, and he takes a large roll of cash and puts it in Josh's hand.*) There you go, your cut.

Josh: What are you talking about? I am going with you to see the buyer.

Jack: No kid, take your cut and go. Permanently. Walk away.

Josh: What?

Jack: I mean it. You will be better off. Okay. Take it from someone who has been in this business. Walk away.

Josh: Wait a minute. Where the hell is this coming from? You were just going on about my talent and how well the job went. Is this some sort of lame ass threat? You brought me in Jack, you introduced me to the circle. Frank, Mikey, Vincent. Don't try to play me now.

Jack: Look, I am not trying to play you, kid. Honest. I like you. I am trying to look out for you. I know what I said, and I know what I have done, but I think maybe I made a mistake... sit down. (*Josh stares intently at Jack, who then motions for him to sit again, and he does.*)

Josh: Good luck finding someone else with my skill.

Jack: I know, but skill isn't all that you have, you have a heart.

Josh: Meaning what?

Jack: Look, I have been in this business a long time. I have seen a lot of different guys come and go, and I see something that is extremely rare to see in you. It's not your just your talent or your brains. You have that, a lot of it, but you also have a heart. A good heart. Inside, you aren't dark. Inside you are not meant for this, kid.

Josh: What are you talking about, man?

Jack: You aren't a criminal. You care. It was a priority for you that no one got hurt, that no blood was spilt. You don't want to kill or hurt anyone, am I right? (*Josh doesn't respond at all.*) Let me tell you something: in this business, you have to be dark. You can't be soft, and you can't have a heart. I know this to be true because, if you do, eventually it gets you killed, or you may as well be dead for the empty shell it will turn you into if you do not have the nature for it. It will isolate you. You will become a shadow just going through motions. You get detached from everyone. I can also promise that if you stay in this business you are going to have to kill. You will have to kill innocence, and first and foremost, you will have to kill all of your own. You are going to cross a line, and either it will kill you or you will embrace it and destroy what is the best part about you.

Josh: Where is this coming from, man? Screw it. (*Getting up.*) You are crazy and, besides, look at you, you don't seem to be destroyed. You are married, you seem decent enough...

Jack: (*Putting Josh up against the wall.*) I'm not joking! I am dead serious, so pay attention to what I have to say. I am a piece of shit, a complete and utter piece of shit. I have done a lot of bad things. I am not a decent person, I am not a good person. I don't care about hurting people or killing people. I have done it before, and I will do it again. You are not like me! (*Releasing his hold on Josh.*) You aren't a piece of shit. You're a good man, but you won't be if you keep doing this. Right now you are able to follow your moral code, but sooner or later that code will have to get thrown out the window, and then something is going to be destroyed. Something worth while is going to get flung as if unwanted and useless into the gutter, and that something is you and your life. It will be the end of you, one way or another. Look kid, I ain't a preacher.

Josh: I'm not too convinced of that right now.

Jack: Look, Josh, you know things about me on the surface. You know how things are perceived, but let me give you a deeper glimpse, and maybe you'll understand a bit better where my point is going. I have been doing "bad" shot for a long time, since your age, since I was a kid. I have been to prisons before, and I have run with rough crowds. I have seen people die, both people I know and people I don't. I have taken lives. I have hurt people, stole from them. I have seen fear, pain, hate and panic in human eyes many times. I have been the cause of those emotions. Do you know what effect that has had on me. Nothing. Every night, I lie down and fall asleep, and I don't feel regret. I don't feel guilt. I don't care at all about what I have done. Do you know why? Because I'm a piece of shit. I am disconnected from people. I just don't care. I do what I want because I can. Do you want to be that? I don't strive to be better or improve. I don't see any mistakes in my life. I am perfectly content to be a low life, miserable piece of shit. Can you honestly tell me inside that you want to have that same title? Look, kid, I know you don't. I know your heart and so do you, whether you want to acknowledge it or not.

135

Josh: If you arte so disconnected, if you are so bad, how are you mar-
            ried? No woman would marry the man you described.

Jack: The world takes all kinds, kid. Look Josh, Betty had no illusions as
            to who or what I was when we got together. She knew my motiva-
            tions from the first night we met. I just wanted to get laid. She
            knows that I will not and do not love her. I am married because she
            wanted me to, but she knows it doesn't impact me in the least.
            Somehow though, just having the husband is worth something to
            her. It isn't like I treat her badly, but she isn't worth more to me
            than myself and my life.

Josh: Why are you telling me all this?

Jack: (*Pauses as if weighing out whether he should tell the truth or not.*)
            Because kid, I like you, for some reason I have a connection to
            you. I never thought I'd have a family. I knew I never wanted kids,
            and Betty didn't either. At first when I met you my interest was
            professional. You have talent. I knew you could make me and the
            other guys money. Now the proof is sitting in my hand. But some-
            thing else occurred in this process of getting to know you. I started
            to see you in a different way. You are on your own, kid, and at first
            I didn't care all that much. (*Pauses.*) Bottom line is that I find my-
            self wanting to look out for you. I want to see you do better than
            me. I may be content with who I am and what I do, but I know it is
            not a good life, and I know I am not a good person. I want you to
            be one, because I can already see that you are, and I don't want you
            to lose it. I see you as a son to me, all right Josh? You are like a
            son, a son I never thought I would have and I thought I would
            never want. Now here you stand and, for one of the first times in
            my life, I have discovered, I give a fuck.

Josh: (*Taking a moment to think and then standing up to look at Jack.*)
            You know I have to call you a liar.

Jack: What do you think I am lying about?

Josh: You said you are a piece of shit. I'd have to disagree. You think I
            am going to ruin myself, and you are trying to stop it. That doesn't
            sound too rotten to me. It actually sounds like a pretty decent per-
            son.

Jack: Well, listen to me. If this is the one "good" thing I do in life, it
            would be a shame if it was wasted. I am a piece of shit; you are just
            an exception to the rule. I'm going to leave now, kid, and you are

going to stay right here. (*Josh goes to speak but Jack stops him.*) No, say nothing, Josh, just stay here. This is where your life begins and mine continues. Be who you really are, and I will continue being the piece of shit I am and will not have to worry about looking out for you and dealing with the fact that there is an exception to rather heartless existence. Good luck.

Jack leaves, and Josh remains. Josh seems to be thinking and sits down on one of the alley crates as the sound of traffic picks up again. The lights go down.

Scene II

The lights come up on a police interrogation room in centre stage. There is a table with two chairs at it. Behind the table sits Jack, and to the left of him stand s a police detective. At the back of the flat, stage right, there is a door.

Detective: Look, Tagan, I know you run with Vincent's gang. You got sloppy, and you got caught. Now you have a couple options. You can do full time, and I'll gladly see that a piece of shit like you gets put where you belong, or you can help us bring down Vincent and his crew. The decision is really all in your hands.

Jack: I am so happy you have left with such wonderful choices, officer. I think I am going to choose option C, where I tell you to go fuck yourself, and then I laugh in your face.

Detective: Hey, if you want to do the time I have no complaints. I'm just trying to do you a favor.

Jack: I'm not a charity case, and I ain't telling you shit. Why don't you go take your ass outside for a walk? You look like you could use it.

Detective: You know, Tagan, you have a chance at redemption here.

Jack: I don't want it, and I don't need it.

Detective: Vincent is a real bad guy.

Jack: So am I. Now fuck off and go eat a doughnut.

Detective: Screw it! I don't need your hard ass routine, cocksucker. You just fucked yourself because your only chance of leniency, me, is walking out the door. (*The detective leaves, and Jack is left on his own sitting in the interrogation room.*)

Jack: I need a smoke. (*At this moment the door to the interrogation room opens, and Josh steps in wearing a suit.*)

Josh: Well hey, Jack, long time no see.

Jack: (*Stunned.*) Josh?

Josh: That's right. What has it been, six years? Want a smoke?

Jack: (*Still in shock, nods, and Josh hands him a cigarette and lights it.*) So, you're a cop?

Josh: Yes I am, I guess it makes our reunion a little bitter, given that it has to be done over this table.

Jack: How did this happen?

Josh: Well, you always said I had talent for being a criminal, and I knew it too. You were also right about me having a heart. So I thought about it and came to a logical conclusion. If I couldn't use my brains and skills to be a criminal, maybe I could use them to catch criminals. It is interesting. It still holds the same thrill and gives me the same rush, and I can feel good about my work. I, like you, can sleep peacefully every night.

Jack: And now you are playing good cop bad cop with me. I am not stupid.

Josh: I know good cop bad cop wouldn't work with you. I actually just thought that I personally may be able to appeal to your better nature.

Jack: What better nature kid? I told you a long time ago that I am a piece of shit.

Josh: And I called you a liar. Look, you can say whatever you want, but I know the truth. You cared about me, you did save me. I know that now. I am asking for your help to take down a guy that is a real piece of shit, unlike you.

Jack: Even if I wanted to help, you can't touch Vincent and his crew.

138

Josh:	We already touched you. Look, I want you to bring me in under-cover. Get me inside his organization, and then we can bring him down. I promise I will look out for you and work to keep you out of prison, or as relaxed of a sentence as I can.
Jack:	You're crazy, kid. You really think I am going to help you? Forget it. My life is what it is, and I am not going to let you screw it up. That's why I got you out of it.
Josh:	You admitted that you cared about me. I know you do. You said I am like a son to you. Despite the hard ass and bad man routine you try to pull, I know it is not the case. You're more of a good person than you want to admit. I think you wanted to save me not just because you saw me like a son, but because you saw some of yourself in me. You wanted to stop me from repeating your mistake. You have a heart too, and I am asking you to use it. I am asking for your help, and if you do it perhaps you will find some peace inside. I know you say you have it, but I don't believe that you do. I think a very large part of you is looking for redemption, and I am going to give it to you.
Jack:	(*Sits quietly for a few moments.*) Fuck you, kid. This is why I wanted you out of my life. I knew if you stayed you'd complicate. Shit. All right, you want my help?
Josh:	Yes, take me in.
Jack:	I hope you realize all that you are asking for. (*The lights go down on the two of them.*)

Scene III

The lights come up on the stage, which is set as the inside of a warehouse. There are various large transport crates and pieces of moving equipment scattered and some chains hang down from the ceiling. It is late at night, and on stage left Jack and Josh are standing and whispering close to each other under one of the warehouse lights.

Jack:	Remember to play this cool.
Josh :	I know, Jack. I've done this before, remember?
Jack:	I know, but if Vincent suspects anything he will more than likely have you killed, and then he'll kill me for bringing you to him.

139

Josh: I got it.

Three men enter from stage right. All of them are well dressed and the man in the middle, Vincent, is wearing all black.

Vincent: Jack, you son of a bitch, how are you?

Jack: Not bad.

Vincent: So, this is the new guy you wanted to introduce me to.

Jack: Yeah, this is him.

Josh: (*Holding out his hand.*) I'm Josh.

Vincent: (*Smiles and takes Josh's hand.*) I know. (*He pulls Josh in close and loses his smile and punches Josh in the stomach.*) You stupid fuck. Grab him. (*Vincent's two men grab a hold of Josh.*)

Josh: What the Hell?!

Vincent: I know you are a cop, and you are trying to bring me in. What a stupid move going after me. (*Grabbing a lead pipe from amongst other items piled by crates in the warehouse.*) What were you thinking, you could just march in here, I'd let you come into my organization, and then you could shut me down from the inside? I was told that you were smart, but this was a truly stupid plan. (*Hits Josh in the stomach with the metal pipe.*)

Josh: Jack?

Thug: Shut up! (*Hitting Josh.*)

Jack: I told you I am a piece of shit.

Vincent: I hope you are ready to die, Josh. I truly hope you are. (*Hitting Josh with the pipe to the ground again.*) Let's go, Jack. You did good today. I promise you'll be rewarded. To think, this idiot used to be on our side. Now he's gonna learn that he should have stayed the hard way. Remember, boys, not to make too much mess.

Thug 2:   Sure thing, boss. (*Jack looks back to Josh on the ground and stops moving.*)

Vincent:	What?
Jack:	I want to stay.
Vincent:	You want to watch?
Jack:	Not exactly. (*Grabbing a gun inside one of Vincent's men's jackets. He points it at Vincent, and the other henchman points his gun at Jack.*)
Vincent:	What the fuck are you doing?
Jack:	Let him go.
Vincent:	Excuse me? You came to me, you told me he was a cop and that he was going to try and infiltrate us undercover. You ratted him out and now, after you have done that, you are deciding to change your mind!
Jack:	I can't really account for my actions or what I am doing now I just have to do it. Get up kid.
Josh:	(*Getting up.*) I'm calling in back up. (*Pulling out a cell phone.*)
Vincent:	The hell you are! (*He pulls a gun and goes to shoot Josh. Jack dives in front of the shot, shooting at Vincent as he does so. Both Jack and Vincent get shot and fall to the ground.*)
Thug:	Let's get the fuck out of here! (*They scatter.*)
Josh:	Oh shit. What a mess. (*Moves over to Jack.*) This is not how things were supposed to go down. Hold on, man, hold on.
Jack:	No, kid. I'm done, and probably better for it.
Josh:	No. No one was supposed to die.
Jack:	I wasn't supposed to betray you to Vincent either. I made a very big mistake.
Josh:	You saved my life.
Jack:	I also almost took it from you. I couldn't, I couldn't let him kill you. It's because…
Josh:	No father could. Once again showing, proving you to be not the

141

piece of shit that you claim to be.

Jack: Enough, kid. I'm already dying. (*He says this with a smile and then his body goes limp and lifeless.*)

Josh is still holding the body as sirens are heard, and the light goes down to being just the alternating red and blue of a police squad light. The detective comes on stage and is looking at Vincent's body. It fades to black while "Sorry seems to be the hardest word" starts playing.

DREAMERS

A note on *Dreamers*

The main point I would like to discuss in this script is the way the characters speak openly and quickly about their lives. Often, we can be guarded, and not be quick to reveal our feelings or our inner truth. I have discovered that often, people, when caught in the right moment, or perhaps with just the right person, have the want if not the need to speak openly and truthfully. I have discovered this tendency with people through working the midnight shifts at Tim Horton's. I have found that, often, whomever I am teamed with at work, we end up speaking a great deal about our lives. It is amazing how wonderful and deep the conversations have gotten with various co-workers of mine. Not only co-workers but also customers have all opened up, and I have opened up to them too. The topics of discussion have gone all over the place. We have talked about goals, dreams, relationships. More importantly, we have revealed weakness or shared vulnerable points with each other. We questioned ourselves through each other and looked for guidance from one another. We could admit shortcomings or failures or help gain a new perspective on a situation in our life we had not seen. There are many discussions I have shared on the midnight shift that I will carry with me and several bonds I created through working on it, which have had an impact on my life. The most important point was it didn't matter our ages, sex, race or background. In that time and place, we were all just people, talking and connecting. If only the world could work that way more often. There are many other points in this brief script that could be discussed, but that was the one I wished to share with you.

Characters

Steve: A stock broker in his early twenties.

Becca: A musician who is beginning her career in her early twenties.

Michael: A homeless man in his early twenties.

Dreamers

The scene opens in a bar where Steve and Becca are sitting. The woman is dressed in jeans and a sweater and is wearing a scarf. She is very pretty. Her hair is put up in an untamed but control fashion. She has a full martini glass in front of her, and she is busy playing with the cherry, which acts as a garnish on the drink. The man is fairly tall and well built. He is dressed well because he judges by appearance and assumes others will do the same. He has a half empty glass in front of him. Both the man and woman seem to be enjoying themselves. There is a blues song playing softly in the background. There is a general feel of depression that often only exists in a bar. It's the kind of sadness that often comes with the mix of booze, overexposed feelings and conversation.

Becca: Where's Michael? He asked us to meet him here.

Steve: It's been years since I've actually seen him, not since high school.

Becca: It's been years since I've seen you, Steve.

Steve: Yeah, too long.

Becca: Seems weird being here.

Steve: How do you mean?

Becca: It's like taking steps back in life, giving you the illusion that you have choices and possibilities again.

Steve: Choices, possibilities, illusions? What are you talking about, Becca?

Becca: Never mind, it's the booze talking.

Steve: You haven't started drinking yet.

Becca looks down quickly at her drink and gives an awkward smile to Steve, and then Michael enters. Michael has a tall and thin frame. He is wearing clothes that were nice once, but he has never known them when they were new. He looks run down and all his movements speak of an inner horror. His presence seems to scream desperation but is nicely placed behind his big smile.

Becca: Michael! (*She says happily and gets up to hug him. She stops cling-*

ing to him, and he quickly turns to Steve, who shakes his hand and wraps his other arm around him.)

Steve: It's good to see you. (*Michael gives an enthusiastic nod, and all three of them sit down. Michael gets a drink and looks back and forth between his two friends with a subtle wonder in his eyes, as if to question if they are real.*) Becca and I were just talking about how long it's been since we've gotten together, all three of us.

Michael: It has been quite a while. You two have changed, but you both look good. (*He pauses, knowing his own looks do not welcome a similar statement.*) So let's catch up. What's been going on with your life, Becca?

Becca: Well, a lot has changed since you saw me last. I'm actually a full-time musician now. I just had a gig last weekend. I was with someone, but it ended kind of messily, so now I'm enjoying being single. I'm making decent money doing what I love. Life is good.

Michael: (*Giving her a penetrating stare while smiling, as if he can tell there is much more for her to say.*) Glad to hear it! What about you, Steve, how is life for you?

Steve: (*Finishing the drink in his glass*) Me, I'm doing well. I finished school and managed to make some wise investment choices, which turned a few heads. Now I'm working with a brokerage firm, and I'm climbing the corporate ladder. I'm making something of myself, just like Becca. (*He says this giving her a smile.*)

Michael: (*Taking a drink from his glass*) That's good, really good. (*Chuckles awkwardly to himself*)

Becca: What about you, Michael? Things must have changed for you.

Steve: Yes, I'm sure you are in a different position than you were in high school.

Michael: The delicate expression of concern (*taking another drink*) Do you remember the night the three of us spent sleeping out in the field at the high school under the stars?

Becca: Yes. It was beautiful.

Steve: Is this why you contacted us in the e-mail? It seemed somewhat strange and urgent. Was it that you just wanted to reminisce? I mean, forgive me for saying this, but by your appearance I doubt you even own a computer.

Michael: You're right, I don't own a computer. I used the library's. In fact, as I am sure you can tell from my appearance, I don't own much, but please bear with me, Steve. Do you remember the night in the field?

Steve: Yes I remember. It was in our first week of grade nine. We called the night our initiation into high school, into real life.

Becca: Gawd, We actually said that we thought high school would reflect real life. (*Takes a drink and looks passively at the glass*)

Michael: Do you remember what we did that night?

Steve: We talked till we fell asleep.

Michael: And what about the stars?

Becca: We wished under them. All of us made a wish and shared it. We said it would be our bond till death.

Steve: We are meeting to talk about our wishes?

Michael: Yes, our wishes for the future, do you remember what you wished?

Becca: I remember I wished to be a musician, to get to create my music my way for my art, to be able to express myself.

Steve: Yeah, I remember the wishes. I wished that I'd get into business, make a fortune and have a family, to have a good life.

Michael: Yes. I wished that we would all be happy. Looks like you two got your wish. You are happy, right? (*Michael looks at the two like he already knows the answer.*)

Becca: Clearly you are having a hard time, Michael, though I am not sure of all the reasons why. But my life isn't so together as it may seem. Look, I have my music, sort of. I'm touring and getting work, always on the move and always busy. I've tried to get some of my own music out, but most of my work is simply covering other famous singers. This isn't as satisfying as I thought it would be. This isn't what I wanted. It's frustrating. Every time I perform, it is not me living my dream, my wish, but rubbing my face that I've come this far but will never go the distance. It just makes me aggra-

149

vated—not even, it makes me angry. My work as a musician just constantly reminds me that I am not good enough. So every performance I do for the rest of my life will help me hate my life just a little bit more. It's depressing. It has pushed me so close to the edge that I pushed away the one good thing I had in my life, Derek. He loved me, and I just let distance grow between us and made him pay for my unhappiness. I took out all of my feelings on him and gave him nothing in return for it. He took it so patiently for so long, Apparently my wish... (*Tears begin to well in her eyes*).

Steve: (*Finishing Becca's statement*) isn't all it was cracked up to be. I know, it's the same for me. I'm in business, but I have no family, and I never will. All I have are the bottoms of empty bottles and glasses to keep me company. So I drink. All I have is built on a lie, a house of cards. I'm the only one who knows it, probably why I drink. My first big deal, my first money maker, it was insider trading. My first and only great deal was illegal. I'm nothing; I'm not the real businessman everyone thinks I am. Every good trade I make feels false, empty. The foundations of all I have and all I am are built on a lie! A lie that consumes all my time, that I try to keep living up to, something I'll have to keep doing for the rest of my life. So there will be no family, because I will have no time, and I am too busy drinking to drown my sorrows to ever think about putting in the effort of living the lie necessary to make the family I wished about. I'm just hollow, and nothing will ever fill me. Be careful what you wish for. (*Gets up to get another drink and sits back down at the table.*) So, Michael, what about you, why don't you bare your soul? It seems to be the trend this evening, and it seems maybe the two of us could appreciate your situation.

Michael: (*Great sadness in his expression*) Appreciate, I can appreciate. Some people talk about rock bottom, but a lot of people never really know what it is. I've always tried to be a good person, to care and help people. I always try to be positive, but I've learned that no matter what you do, reality, life, will get the better of you. I brought a person in need into my life, and it destroyed it. I started working right after high school, in a job as an office assistant. I loved my job and my bosses. I met this woman at a bar, she was crying and I went to her because I could see her pain. Her name was Amy. I started falling for her, and I let her move in. Then she ended up robbing me. She was mixed up with Meth, and apparently I wasn't the only one she robbed. She robbed her dealer and, in retaliation, he decided to burn her house, my house. I found her, OD in an ally. I had no cash, no home and because of my connection to all of these shady events, I soon had no job. I was played, hurt and left with nothing. I've gotten a new job at McDonalds. What a shining achievement! I'm barely scraping by, living at a shelter. I needed a pick me up, so I decided I'd find the two of you, hopefully living your dreams and being happy. Then I could borrow a little of your happiness.

Steve: Now you contact us, and you find we're no better off than you.

All three stare at their empty glasses.

Becca: I miss high school, I miss the illusions. I miss being happy.

Steve: Let's get out of here; it's depressing. (*The three leave the bar, and the lights go down on the set and come up on a lone street lamp where the three are now standing.*) Well Michael, I'd say it's been a lovely evening but...

Michael: Yeah.

Steve: (*Moving closer and giving him a hug*) It was good to see you.

Michael: You too.

Becca: (*Hugging Michael*) I hope things get better. (*She lets go of him, and she and Steve start to walk away.*)

Michael: They will. I know they will. I have a confession. (*The other two stop moving.*) I have been watching the two of you for a little while. I knew you were unhappy, or I felt you were. (*Tears are starting, and he's having a hard time.*) I asked you to come here tonight to confirm my suspicions, so I could make you happy. So I could make your dreams and mine come true.

Steve: (*Clearly nervous*) What do you mean, Michael? Are you all right?

Becca: (*Soothing*) Michael, relax it's okay.

Michael: I know. (*He pulls out a gun and shoots both of them, one shot each. He starts crying and goes and kneels by the bodies.*) I just wanted us to all be happy, to be free, to live our dreams. You dream when you sleep. Now you'll sleep, now you'll dream. You're happy. Now you're happy. (*Michael gets up and starts walking. He is completely shattered and walks as if in a trance, all sense of reality is lost. Then he begins to sing softly.*) When you wish upon a star, makes no difference who you are, when you wish upon a star, your dreams come true. (*The lights go down, and one final gun shot is heard.*)

ETHICS

A note on *Ethics*

This is a script I really enjoyed writing. The subject of human morality is one that has always interested me, and I have always been interested in the extremes and the abilities of people to rise to a moral and ethical hero or to sink to the bottom of the ethical slime pool. There is no need to name names, and I am sure you can insert a great many to that statement. It is amazing to see in just everyday life how many people will do what's right. Mind you, a large part of this is also based on whether a particular person's concept of right is actually right. Mind you, I don't want to get too philosophical with it right now.

An example I can give from my personal life is something I will do at Tim Hortons. I will, at times, give more than the proper change back to see if anyone will be honest and inform me of the apparent mistake. I have done this several times, and only once has anyone ever corrected me. It actually makes me a little sad and disappointed inside. Don't worry, though, I am not a hypocrite, I use my tips and sometimes my own cash to replace whatever extra went out of the till. It is just one of those experiments that intrigues me.

I find that this script and story has a lot to say about ethics on many levels, from the arguments of the characters to analyzing the ethics of the method of teaching the play's professor employs. Or, you can break the fourth wall and look at what the script has included in it, and question whether it is ethical, or making an argument against some of the points that the characters in the script might argue are ethical. It is a large web and, I hope, a fun read. It is a play I look forward to producing, and I am sure I will produce it sooner rather than later. I hope it entertains and perhaps makes you pause to think about ethics in the world around us and maybe even those that you hold inside yourself.

Characters

Sarah Wilkens:
>A first year University student who has undergone a personality transformation over the past year. She cares first and foremost about herself and will allow this to influence her life decisions, which are starting to take a self-destructive turn that could ruin her life or end it.

Dr. Malcolm:
>A brilliant and controversial ethics professor who has an almost dangerous passion for his work.

Tran: A sadistic and cruel drug dealer and criminal.

Brendan: Sarah's boyfriend, who is oblivious to the dark areas of Sarah's life and does not realize who she truly is.

Melissa: Sarah's roommate and friend, who is devastated to see what Sarah is doing to herself and the people around her.

Ethics

Act I

Scene I

The stage is set into a dorm room in a university residence. There are two beds and a desk with laptops on it. Two girls are in the room. One is lying on the bed, and the other is sitting in the chair at the desk. In between the two beds in the flat is a door for the closet. Sarah, the girl on the bed, looks a bit strung out and is dressed in a short leather skirt and a tight fitting, low-cut top. Her hair is a little wild, and she has an intense and fiery look in her eyes. The other girl, Melissa, is sitting just staring at Sarah and clearly is not impressed with her. She is dressed more casually, perhaps even a bit on the preppy side. There is loud metal music playing on the stereo, and Melissa turns it off, clearly annoyed.

Melissa: Okay, Sarah, I am just going to come out and say it. What the fuck are you doing?! Look at yourself.

Sarah: *(Sitting up.)* Wow. Quiet girl can swear. What the hell has you so upset?

Melissa: You, Sarah, you do. Look what has happened to you. Look at where you are. I remember when we used to laugh at the beginning of the year. We had fun. Now you have been making a wreck of yourself.

Sarah: Oh, really. Do explain how I have been ruining my life—because I have a social life instead of being buried in my books? I have money; is that my problem? Maybe it is my boyfriend, Brendan. Maybe he is ruining my life. Funny how all those things are things that you do not have.

Melissa: While I don't think he is a great guy, I don't think he is part of your problems and, it is not jealousy which is spurring my remarks.

Sarah: Listen, I don't need a lecture, and I don't need your bullshit. If you have something to say, just come out and say it.

Melissa: Fine. Let's see. Since the beginning of the year, you have managed to gain a boyfriend, constantly lie to that boyfriend, get a job as a private dancer at a strip club, start using cocaine, start selling cocaine for Tran... I think there is a problem, Sarah.

Sarah: Well Melissa, let's review facts. I met Brendan, and we started going out. Then I needed money. I needed a job, and I couldn't find work anywhere. If I recall, it was you who suggested that I try stripping.

Melissa: I was joking. I told you that the very first time I said it.

Sarah: There is nothing wrong with it.

Melissa: Hey, if you are fine with it and it makes you cash, then so be it. What I don't like is that you know Brendan would hate it, and you have the nerve to say you care about him, maybe even love him, and you lie to him!

Sarah: I don't intend to lose him, and if he knew I would.

Melissa: So stop.

Sarah: No, it is good money. Not to mention it is how I get sales done for Tran, and I get a decent cut.

Melissa: Tran is just a fuck head! I hate him. You were so much sweeter before he got you into cocaine. Now you have just become a bitch. It has seriously screwed you up, Sarah.

Sarah: (*Standing up to intimidate Melissa.*) Watch your mouth! This is my life, and I am living it. I am getting ahead.

Melissa: You are losing your head! (*Starting to tear up.*) Don't you see. Sarah? I care about you, you are my friend, I love you. (*Grabs an old picture of the two of them.*) Look, see? I want us to be like this again. I want you back. I want you back.

Sarah: (*Taking the picture and sitting down on the bed.*) Things have changed. But I don't mind change. I have Brendan, I am getting through school, and now I am going to be making a lot more money with this. (*Produces a brick of cocaine from under her bed.*)

Melissa: Where did you get that?

Sarah: From Tran. I ripped it off of him, and now I am going to sell it myself.

158

Melissa:	Oh my God, Sarah, you are going to get yourself killed!
Sarah:	You are being too dramatic. Tran won't notice. I'm smarter than that.
Melissa:	If the state of your life is any indication of your intelligence, then you are the dumbest girl to ever walk this Earth.
Sarah:	(*Clearly getting very upset.*) Are you done, Melissa? Clearly it doesn't matter what I have to say, because you are not going to listen to my justifications.
Melissa:	There is nothing to justify. You are screwing up and for yourself and your life you need to change it.
Sarah:	Fuck you, bitch! (*Getting up to leave.*) Enjoy your books.
Melissa:	(*Grabbing hold of Sarah.*) Wait. Please talk to me.
Sarah:	(*Shaking Melissa off.*) Screw you! (*Leaves stage left.*)
Melissa:	You need help!
Sarah:	(*Offstage.*) And you need to get laid! (*The lights go down on the stage.*)

Scene II

The stage is still set as the dorm room. The lights come on, and Melissa is lying on the bed with her eyes open and blood running from her mouth and on the bed sheets. The brick of cocaine is sitting up beside her dead body. Sarah comes in, stumbling slightly, and takes a glance at Melissa. The she looks harder again and rushes over to her, clearly panicking and upset, fruitlessly trying to revive her. As she does the closet door opens, and Tran steps out. He is an intimidating figure with a sadistic grin, purple tinted shades and a shaved head.

Tran:	You can work on her all night. It won't do any good.
Sarah:	(*Turning around, startled.*) Tran…
Tran:	Yeah, Miss sexy Sarah. That's me. (*Sits down on the bed and pulls out a knife.*) She was a bleeder.

159

Sarah:	You bastard, you did this?! Fucker! (*She goes to leap at him, but he holds out the knife threateningly, and she relaxes.*)
Tran:	That's what I thought. I kill your friend, but your life is more important than that. You're a survivor.
Sarah:	Why did you do it? What did she do to you?
Tran:	Nothing. It's what you did.
Sarah:	What?
Tran:	Right there. (*Pointing to the stolen cocaine on the bed.*) You stole from me, Sarah. I don't appreciate that. Now, your friend had to pay for your sins.
Sarah.	(*Holding Melissa's head and crying into her hair.*) She said I was going to kill myself.
Tran:	Nope, just her. (*He moves over to Sarah and grabs her by the arm. He pulls her away from Melissa and flings her onto the other bed.*) Sit down. We need to have a talk. (*He sits down beside the cocaine and Melissa's body.*) Robbing from me is a very serious offence, and you are going to have to pay very dearly for it. I am not a very forgiving person, but I am going to give you a chance to live, and I think you'll take it, because you are a survivor.
Sarah:	(*Very nervous.*) What do you mean?
Tran:	I'm going to make you do things, Sarah. If you live up to my expectations and complete the tasks, then you will live. If you don't, then you will die. It is as simple as that.
Sarah:	What tasks?
Tran:	I am so glad you asked. You see, these tasks are about punishment. I'll be honest when I say I am going to torture you. (*Back hands her across the face.*) That you just had coming to you.
Sarah:	What do you want me to do?
Tran:	First, I want you to take this phone. (*Picks up her cell phone on the desk*) And I want you to call your boyfriend.

160

Sarah:	Why do you want me to call him?
Tran:	I want you to not just call him but to invite him over. I want the two of you to get together and have a chat. I want you to tell him about some of your extra curricular activities. I want you to admit how long you have been working as a private dancer behind his back. So go ahead, dial the number and have him over.
Sarah:	What are you going to do?
Tran:	Me? Oh, I am just going to hang out in the closet. I thought I'd stick around and listen. I thought it could be a lot of fun. Go on, dial the number.
Sarah:	What about Melissa?
Tran:	Don't worry. After you call, we're going to go and move her to my trunk. I'll make her disappear later. Leave the drugs, though. I think you should explain those to him too, explain how you have been selling them and stealing them. Of course, mention my name or word one about me being around, and I'll kill him, and then I will kill you. He'll be first though, so you can watch.
Sarah:	(*On the verge of breaking down.*) You're a bastard!
Tran:	(*Leaning in close with the knife.*) I'm just getting started. Now call.

Scene III

The stage is set as the dorm room. The bed has been cleaned up, and Melissa's body is gone. Tran is nowhere to be seen, and the drugs are sitting on the desk. Sarah is wiping tears away from her face and rocking on the bed. There is a knock, and she goes off-stage and comes back on with Brendan walking in behind her.

Brendan:	(*Upon seeing Sarah's state.*) What's wrong, honey? What's going on? You sounded shook up on the phone.
Sarah:	(*Trying to gain composure.*) Brendan, do you love me?
Brendan:	Yes, of course, what is it?
Sarah:	I have some things that I have to tell you.
Brendan:	Like what?

161

Sarah: (*Pausing, struggling to find the words.*) I haven't been honest with you.

Brendan: What do you mean? (*Notices the cocaine on the desk*) What is this?

Sarah: That's part of it.

Brendan: You're doing coke.

Sarah: And selling it.

Brendan: What are you thinking?!

Sarah: It just happened.

Brendan: (*Picking up the drugs and turning on Sarah.*) Where did you get the money to afford this?

Sarah: I didn't. (*Beginning to cry.*) I didn't .I stole it.

Brendan: Oh, shit. Sarah! You stole this. From who?

Sarah: My dealer.

Brendan: So are you in trouble. Does he know?

Sarah: I think he does.

Brendan: (*Sitting down by her and trying to calm her.*) Look, we'll make this all right. Where did you meet a coke dealer?

Sarah: At my job.

Brendan: What job? You told me months ago you couldn't find one.

Sarah: Remember when I asked you about working at the strip club?

Brendan: (*Moving away from her slightly.*) The one I said I didn't want you working at.

Sarah: Yes, well, I went and I got a job there, as a private dancer.

Brendan: (*Standing up.*) You what?

Sarah: I know you didn't want me to.

Brendan: You're damn right, I didn't.

Sarah: I just wanted the money, so I took the job.

Brendan: And then you wanted coke, so you started buying it, and then you wanted more money, so you started selling it. Then I suppose you wanted more money, so you stole some to sell and take the profit yourself, all the while lying to me and telling me nothing. Who the fuck are you?!

Sarah: I'm the girl you just said a few minutes ago that you love.

Brendan: That was before I found out how much you have been lying to me and hiding from me.

Sarah: I didn't want to.

Brendan: But you just did. Save it.

Sarah: Look, I want to make it up to you.

Brendan: Make it up to me? You can't make it up to me, Sarah. I can not forgive this.

Sarah: You could if you loved me?

Brendan: The Sarah I love would never do this, but it seems the Sarah I love is nothing more than a figment of my imagination. I guess I need to grow up and lose my imaginary friend.

Sarah: Are you saying we're over?

Brendan: We never started. All I see in front of me is a lying, twisted coke head.

Sarah: I can't believe you are saying that. You bastard! I thought you loved me.

Brendan: I'm a bastard?! Let's reverse the roles for a minute. What would you be saying to me if it were me who came in here and told you all of these things? How would you feel? (*Sarah is silent.*) That's what I thought.

Sarah: Couldn't you just let me explain?

Brendan: There is nothing to explain. We are through.

Sarah: (*Grabbing Brendan's arm.*) Wait! Don't go. (*She pulls him close and kisses him, and he shoves her off.*)

Brendan: Get off me.

Sarah: Son of a bitch! (*She slaps him.*)

Brendan: (*Spins around in anger and hits Sarah and knocks her to the ground. He realizes what he has done, and there is pain in his eyes. He moves to help her and then stops. He moves toward stage left, and he looks back.*) Stay away from me. (*He exits, and Tran moves out from the closet while Sarah is still on the floor, whimpering.*)

Tran: Tisk. Tisk. What a shame to see young lovers fight.

Sarah: Go fuck yourself.

Tran: It looks like he hit you pretty hard. Would you like to hit him back?

Sarah: (*Looking up, a mix of confusion and fear on her face.*) What do you mean?

Tran: Well, I don't think you are done hurting him yet.

Sarah: No, I am not going to do anything else to him. He is innocent.

Tran: Yes he is, but you are not. Once again the innocent will suffer for your sins. Is it getting to you yet?

Sarah: You are a sick son of a bitch.

Tran: (*Smiling.*) I know. So what do you say? Shall we continue, or do you want to take the noble way out and offer yourself up for death?

Sarah: (*Emotionally struggling.*) What do you want me to do?

Tran: Well, I think it is clear that Brendan needs to die. But I am not going to be the one to do it. You are.

Sarah: (*Beginning to break down again.*) No...

Tran: (*Moving closer and holding her.*) Yes, yes, yes. I think we'll make

164

it poetic too. Tonight you will go to work at the club. I will go find Brendan, and I'll get him drunk and drug him up. Then, in a stupor, I will bring him to your private dancing booth at the club. I'll give you a knife and send him in and, as long as he doesn't come out, you can, and you will be able to continue with your life, or what is left of it.

Sarah: I hate you. I fucking hate you.

Tran: What a shame. I thought we were bonding. I will see you at the club tonight. If you don't show, it just means that you will both be dying. (*Takes a picture of Brendan and Sarah together off of her desk.*) Here, kiss him goodbye before you send him away. (*He exits, and Sarah is left on the floor on stage and hurls the picture away, smashing the glass on the front of it, and begins to cry in pain, misery and anger as the lights go out.*)

Scene IV

The stage is now set to be the private dancing booth in the club that Sarah works at. There is a chair centre stage and a door on stage left. She is scantily dressed and has a boa. There is dance music playing softly in the background, and it gets louder as Tran opens the door and enters and then quiets as he shuts the door.

Tran: So, are you ready for your big performance? I'm about to send in your client.

Sarah: Fuck you.

Tran: (*Pulling out a knife and running it down her body.*) Careful, or I may change my mind about this being your last test. Here you go. (*Hands her the knife.*) Don't get any funny ideas. (*Revealing a gun in his belt.*) Now remember, the client that I send in cannot leave this room.

Sarah: The client?

Tran: Oh yes, one final surprise. I didn't pick up Brendan. I found some-one else. Someone you know, someone innocent. They're drunk and drugged, and I will be sending them in shortly. The same rules still apply. They cannot leave. I hope you fully understand.

Sarah: No I can't, I won't.

Tran: (*Pulling the gun.*) Then you'll die! What do you think, survivor? Is it time to go?

Sarah: (*Pauses for a moment.*) Send him in.

Tran: That's what I like to see, ready and willing. If nothing else, you know you love yourself. Whatever fucked up bitch you see staring back in the mirror at you, you do love her. (*Tran leaves.*)

Sarah: (*Voiceover through the sound system while she is getting ready.*) I don't know who I am any more. I haven't known for a while. (*The door opens, and a man dressed sloppily in a suit and clearly having had too much to drink enters the room. He is older, and Sarah recognizes him instantly*) That's Dr. Malcolm, my ethics professor. Oh my God. I can't do this. I have to do this. He's going to kill me. (*To Dr. Malcolm.*) Take a seat, Sir.

Malcolm: You sure are beautiful.

Sarah: Thank you. (*Putting him in the chair.*)

Sarah: (*A voiceover once again as a new piece of music starts playing, and she begins to dance very erotically in front of the professor.*) I can't believe what I am doing. This is so wrong. He is a good man, brilliant. I can't go through with this. (*She begins to strip out of her clothes and becomes topless.*) But if I don't, Tran will kill me, and I do not want to die. (*She begins moving around the chair and then pulls out the knife and runs it down the front of her body. She runs it down Dr. Malcolm, who sees it all as part of the show.*) I have to do this. I hope he can forgive me. I have to, but at least I can give him a good show before he goes. (*She climbs up onto his lap and straddles him on the chair. She moves in close and continues to dance on him, using the knife as a prop in an erotic fashion.*) I have to do it now. (*She goes to strike and, as she does, the professor becomes fully alert and tosses her off him and onto the floor.*) What's going on?! (*The professor pulls out a gun and points it at her.*) What is this, NO! (*The lights go out, she screams, and there is a gun shot.*)

Act II

Scene I

The lights come on, and the stage is now set as a lecture hall in the university. Sarah is sitting at a desk, dressed as she was in the pictures Melissa had from her at the beginning of the year. She has no hardness about her. She seems happy and sweet. In front of her, at a podium, stands Dr. Malcolm in a suit and he looks very alert, lively and focused.

Malcolm: Good morning class, welcome to ethics. I am certain there are a number of you sitting here today who are very unsure of why you are taking this class. Perhaps some of you heard that this is an easy credit, but I assure you that this is not the case when I teach it. Personally, I feel that ethics should be a requirement, not just for students and academics, but for all people and for life. It is not just a simple question of what is right or wrong, but a question of how people should live and treat each other. I firmly believe that if we lived in a more ethical world we would live in a far better one.

Now, how do I mean this? Well, let us look at some examples. Business, for example, I am sure many of you plan to enter into this field. Can you imagine a world where businesses actually act ethically? I am sure some of you are looking at me, thinking I am just too liberal, or that I am a product of the 60's. Both I feel are untrue. Imagine a business that gives a shit, one that cares about how it is affecting the lives of those around it, a company that cares if its employees are dying due to unsafe conditions or if children are being forced to work like slaves, a company that cares to pay fair wages and will not allow lives to be lost in the name of profit, or even a company that can be honest with its consumer and tell them the truth about the products they are buying. It's a novel idea, I know.

Or imagine a world where politicians actually talk straight and fairly. Wouldn't that be an incredible sight to see? Where they tell what they will do and they treat the voters with respect? Maybe we would even get more voters turning out to vote, because they might feel lie it will mean something, that it can actually count, because honesty and straightforwardness are qualities the government actually holds onto. Maybe the idea of honesty and ethics would even flow to the news and media and, for the first time, we might receive real news because now the corporations, being ethical, have taken their strangle hold off of it, and the politicians have too. It would be the first time a fair, unbiased and appropriate news story hits in years.

Are you all starting to understand how ethics could create a major change, the importance it can hold to you and your future? Well, we can give it a test. You, miss, in the front row, what will ethics do for you?

Sarah: I...uhhh

Malcolm: I...uhhh would not be a very useful answer. Want to try again?

Sarah: It helps us live better. It will help us be better people.

Malcolm: In my eyes it will, but that doesn't make it a truth. Ultimately, what ethics will do is define you.

Sarah: How do you mean, it defines us?

Malcolm: It makes a statement about who you are and where you will fit in the world and among the people around you.

Sarah: So are you saying we are being judged?

Malcolm: Young lady, the whole world is always judging you. Every person you meet is judging you. It is the reality of our world. People are meant to be judged and categorized. It is the reality of our world. (*Pause.*) This class will be no exception. All of you will be tested before it is through, and we will see just how much you have learned about ethics and, more importantly, about your own.

Sarah: So, we are going to be judged by your standards then.

Malcolm: Well, obviously. This is a university class, and I am the professor. Obviously I am judging you. But I will not be the last. This is one class and a set of lessons that you will continue to be judged on and by for your entire life. So I encourage you to take it seriously and give it some thought. This is more than just about learning how to be good and responsible people. It is about your life and helping determine where it could go and what you could be. Your ethics will become responsible for who you are and what you become in your eyes and the eyes of others. That is all for today. (*The lights fade.*)

Scene II

The stage is set to be a private meeting room with a table and various people sitting around it. There are some file folders with Sarah's picture on them and in them are various other forms and papers. Dr. Malcolm is sitting behind the table, and sitting with him are Melissa, Brendan and Tran. They are dressed in plain street clothes and are flipping through the files and photos.

Malcolm: The next student is Sarah Wilkens, and you three will be the ones primarily interacting with her. I have gotten all of you strategically positioned so as to be able to play your roles and influence or suggest various situations to her. I hope the three of you are up for playing more long-term roles.

Brendan: How long?

Malcolm: Several months, I would say.

Tran: By this outline, she needs to start working at the strip club before I would even begin to interact with her.

Malcolm: Yes, and I am quite certain she will have done this before, and it tends to play out that way.

Melissa: So, explain this whole thing out to me a little bit again.

Malcolm: Certainly. I have discovered the best way to teach students about ethics is to show them their own. I do this by putting their ethics to the test. More often than not, this leads to a downward spiral that destroys their life, or it would if it were real. I hire you as actors to take on roles that you will play: her roommate, boyfriend, etc. We will direct her towards certain choices and see where they take her. We will keep pushing her and see just how low she can go, and when she can go no lower, then we give her a wake up call.

Melissa: So, I am supposed to nudge her towards the stripping job.

Malcolm: Yes, once she has hooked up with our resident stud over here. (*Pointing to Brendan.*) Of course, he will be dead set against it, but we'll see if she is willing to hide it from him. Then we'll have Tran enter. You'll begin presenting her with option of trying cocaine and hiding that, and then push her to sell. See what she does next.

Tran: Dr. Malcolm, you realize that cocaine is illegal, that doing this involves us all in criminal actions.

Malcolm: Anyone she sells to will be a plant. Anyone who uses it save for her will be a plant. These projects I put the students through are elaborate but costly.

Brendan: Either you are a genius, or you are just crazy.

Malcolm: They often go hand in hand.

Melissa: So, you have a stash of cocaine for this.

Malcolm: Correct.

Tran: And you do this with all of your students?

Malcolm: Not the exact same scenarios, but similar ideas. Each student is tested and has their life influenced by actors. You are my pawns, to see what sort of ethical decisions the students will make for themselves.

Brendan: How do you grade this?

Malcolm: I don't. This is just a time for real learning to take place on behalf of the student. The lesson I will teach them with this is one that they will carry for the rest of their life. I give them a whole second chance with their ethics and life even before they truly ruined the first one. They can see how far they may fall and not have to truly face the consequences. They only have to face themselves. I will admit that that can be the hardest but most valuable part of the project. I always like to be there for that moment. Giving the right wake up call is the most important part.

Scene III

The stage is set to the private dance booth in the club. Sarah is still lying on the ground, and Dr. Malcolm is standing above her with the gun. She is shielding her body like she has been shot, and the dance music is playing in the background. Dr, Malcolm puts the gun away and tosses Sarah's top to her.

Malcolm: Relax. You are not dead. It was a blank. In fact, I have a few bits of relieving news for you.

Sarah: What?

Malcolm: Yes, Sarah, a great deal of what you believe has happened to you hasn't really happened to you. You have not stolen from a drug dealer or really sold drugs to people, just people I have plated for you to do so. You have not really lied to your boyfriend or betrayed someone you loved, because he was an actor I planted. Your roommate has not been killed, because she was another actor and was pretending to be dead with the help of some drugs to slow the heart and make her breathing practically undetectable. Furthermore, Tran is not really a drug dealer, and you are not actually caught in a sadistic game. He is another actor, and you have just completed your project for my ethics class.

Sarah: I have what? I am so confused. (*Beginning to cry.*)

Malcolm: It's all right, let it out. Often students have to. You have been through a lot all semester long. It was all a set up, designed to reveal to you your true personal ethics. Don't worry, this project is not being marked. It is simply for your learning experience. You have seen where your ethics can take you, and now it is up to you to decide what you should do with that knowledge.

Sarah: So Tran, Brendan, Melissa, my life—all fake.

Malcolm: For this semester they are. (*Picks Sarah up and sits her down.*) I warned you on the first day of class that ethics wasn't easy when I teach it. My methods are unique. Though I am certain you have truly learned something from this. Remember it and remember it well. I have no doubt that this will be one of the most important lessons you will ever learn. (*He exits out of the private dance room and leaves Sarah alone.*)

Sarah: (*As a voiceover while she sits crying on the chair in a spot light.*) It was the hardest lesson I ever learned. Nothing about it was easy or simple. I learned more about myself than I ever would have thought and more than I ever would have wanted to know. I learned from it. I knew what it felt like to make those mistakes, and I was not planning to make them again. I learned the hard way and, although Dr. Malcolm's methods were harsh, controversial and possibly dangerous, they worked. I have a clear picture when I look in the mirror. I know now how I will be judged. I know what I would have done, and from knowing that I managed to make myself a new. I got a chance to get it wrong so I could get it right. Now I smile when I look in the mirror. (*To the audience.*) Can you? (*Lights go out on her, and a spot goes on Dr. Malcolm, downstage left.*)

Malcolm: Class dismissed. (*Lights go out, and curtain closes.*)

www.ingramcontent.com/pod-product-compliance
Lightning Source LLC
Chambersburg PA
CBHW070759100426
42742CB00012B/2197